Other *Yale Daily News* Guides from Kaplan Books

Yale Daily News *Guide to Fellowships and Grants*

Yale Daily News *Guide to Succeeding in College*

Yale Daily News *Working Knowledge*

OLDEST COLLEGE DAILY   FOUNDED JANUARY 28, 1878

Guide to Writing College Papers

By Justin M. Cohen

Marti Page

and the staff of the *Yale Daily News*

Simon & Schuster

NEW YORK · LONDON · SINGAPORE · SYDNEY · TORONTO

Kaplan Publishing
Published by Simon & Schuster
1230 Avenue of the Americas
New York, NY 10020

Contributing Editor: Trent Anderson
Project Editor: Donna Ratajczak
Cover Design: Cheung Tai
Interior Page Design: Michael Shevlin
Interior Page Production: Jean Cohn
Production Editor: Maude Spekes
Production Manager: Michael Shevlin
Managing Editor: Dave Chipps
Executive Editor: Del Franz

Special thanks to: Beth Grupper and Sara Pearl.

For bulk sales to schools, colleges, and universities, please contact: Order Department, Simon and Schuster, 100 Front Street, Riverside, NJ 08075. Phone: 1-800-223-2336. Fax: 1-800-943-9831.

Manufactured in the United States of America
Published simultaneously in Canada

September 2000
10 9 8 7 6 5 4 3 2 1

ISBN: 0-684-87345-1

TABLE OF CONTENTS

ABOUT THE AUTHORS

Justin Cohen is a molecular, cellular, and developmental biology major at Yale University, although he is considering a double major in procrastination and poor time management. When he is not recording with Rocinante, his soon-to-be *Billboard* chart-topping band, or writing books about writing, he enjoys cross-country running, fine wines, and long walks on the beach. In the future, Justin hopes to author a new book, possibly a guide to writing books about writing.

Marti Page is majoring in American studies at Yale University. When she is not throwing water balloons at people who walk past her dorm room window, slaving over one of the seventeen papers her loving professors have assigned during the school year, or writing convoluted sentences (like this one), she acts as a Yale tour guide and executive editor of the *Yale Daily News Insiders' Guide to College*. Marti is involved in Bible studies and enjoys brief stints with the Yale Women's Crew Team.

ACKNOWLEDGMENTS

The authors would like to thank all of the students and professors who contributed their advice to this book (without whom there would be many blank pages), the publishers of the *Yale Daily News* (without whom the book would have been completed several months quicker), and, of course, all those students who failed to follow through on their threats to sue us for harassment and solicitation (without whom life would be far less interesting).

OLDEST COLLEGE DAILY · FOUNDED JANUARY 28, 1878

Founded on January 28, 1878, the *Yale Daily News* is the oldest college daily paper in the United States. The all-student staff publishes a 10- to 16-page newspaper five nights a week, reporting stories related to the Yale and New Haven communities. Financially independent from the university, the *Yale Daily News* supports its own production through student-sold advertising.

Boasting an alumni list that includes Henry Luce, Sargent Shriver, Potter Stewart, William F. Buckley Jr., Garry Trudeau, Calvin Trillin, and Shelley Fisher Fishkin, the *Yale Daily News* has been called the best unofficial undergraduate school of journalism. Today's *Yale Daily News* remains committed to the mission of teaching journalism, conducting skills workshops, and hosting alumni speakers.

In addition to the daily newspaper, the *Yale Daily News* publishes a weekly news magazine, a monthly compilation of stories, and the *Insider's Guide to the Colleges*—a guidebook to the nation's colleges created by interviewing current undergraduates.

Most recently, the *Yale Daily News* has entered a joint venture with Kaplan Books and Simon & Schuster to produce a series of guide books to assist and advise students throughout their college careers. Titles include *Yale Daily News Guide to Succeeding in College*, *Yale Daily News Guide to Fellowships and Grants*, *Yale Daily News Guide to Internships*, and this publication. Authored by staff members of the *Yale Daily News*, all the books offer valuable tips for college success drawn from the experiences of actual students.

INTRODUCTION

Rumor has it that a particular Yale professor graces his students' papers with especially cruel comments. According to the tale, one hapless freshman named Jane Doe submitted what she considered a well-written paper to her prominent and respected English lecturer. Upon receiving the graded paper, however, our freshman eagerly flipped to the last page, where she was dismayed to read her professor's sole comment: "ADMISSIONS ERROR."

Ouch. Maybe you're a first-year student, entering college with trepidation and a fear of reading comments even more "constructive" than Jane Doe's. Maybe your mother bought this book for you on sale and told you that you wouldn't get your allowance unless you read it in its entirety. Maybe you're waiting for your dentist appointment, and this book is the only reading material in sight.

Regardless of your motive, we're glad to see you. What you're about to read is a book about writing—for college students, by college students. We've survived our share of papers, managed to convince our parents to raise our allowance, and had our cavities filled. Our dentist, however, subscribes to *Field and Stream* (if you want a referral, call us later).

Sure, we have our own stories to tell, but college writing is too broad to be encompassed by the advice of your lowly authors. In writing this book, we've attempted to compile a diverse and realistic collection of student experiences. But wait . . . here's more—to try to give you the whole story, we've also asked the professors, writing tutors, and TAs (in other words, the people who grade your papers) to contribute the techniques they like best and the errors they dislike most.

Introduction

Throughout the book, we'll try to present the ideal process for completing a typical paper. Let's be honest: We don't always follow each step to the letter, and we don't expect that you always will either. We understand that your afternoons are filled with sousaphone practice, your nights are dedicated to calling the *Who Wants to Be a Millionaire* hotline, and your weekends are spent driving to tiddledywinks tournaments—and that's not even including last Thursday's twenty-four-hour Moonwalk-a-thon to benefit homeless wombats.

The point is that we understand. We'll be here for you. But don't think we're going to let you slack off. Just because you can't do everything exactly the way the experts recommend doesn't mean you can't produce a paper that even the most critical of professors will read with approval.

We'll lead you through the whole process, with tips from students and professors, and inspirational quotes. We've also included a hundred or so unusual words with definitions, which you'll notice at the bottom of every other page. We don't recommend using them in your papers, but you can always work them into conversations with your friends. So let's start at the beginning . . .

Chapter One

GETTING STARTED

You clipped your fingernails. You cleaned your room. You even subjected yourself to watching *The View*.

At some point, even the staunchest of procrastinators has no choice but to fire up the computer and knock out that ten-page assignment.

The actual process of writing a paper is almost never as daunting a task as it appears at the outset. The hard part is getting started. A blank page can be far more intimidating than the actual paper assignment.

> As for getting started—often the most difficult thing for a writer—there is one piece of information that has always made my writing process easier: No matter how long you've been writing, it never really gets any easier. I have been writing full time for nearly 10 years and I sweat blood every single time I sit down in front of a blank page to begin a story. But somehow, knowing that many writers, no matter how seasoned, face this same dilemma makes me feel better!
>
> —Jordan Smith, freelance writer, master's candidate at the University of Texas—Austin

FINDING A TOPIC (or Without a Purpose Your Paper Is Worthless)

The first, but by no means the easiest, task in front of the paper writer is to select a topic for the future masterpiece. If the subject of the paper is assigned by the professor, this shouldn't be a head-scratcher. Read the question and see what it tells you to do. Professors vary in the amount of direction they give. Some will give guidelines, while others prefer that the student think of a topic independently.

> Chance favors the prepared mind.
> —Louis Pasteur

> Read the essay assignment. You wouldn't believe how many times I've written on the wrong subject or forgotten key aspects of an essay.
> —Brad Olson, Harvard, government major

> When students are asked to write a response to a multipart question, they often fail to address all the parts in their response.
> —Lynn Marie Hoffman, Professor of Education, Bucknell University

Really read the question, several times. Scrutinize it, comprehend it, interpret it. Look for those key words that tell you what the professor's looking for. Does it say *argue* or *analyze*? (See below for the difference.) How about: *criticize, define, describe, discuss, evaluate, explain, reflect on,* or *summarize*?

If the professor's a nice person, he or she might throw you some bones—hints as to what to include, specific topics, that sort of thing. Write those down right away so they'll make it into your outline.

> If you have a choice on topics, pick one that truly interests you. Not only will it not seem like as much work, but you will accomplish the goal of the paper: You will learn.
> —Susan Reynolds, American studies major/art history minor

abecedarian: teacher of the alphabet; *adj* alphabetically arranged

The Sooner You Start . . . and Other Tips

Smaller goals are a great help. Make them realistic and in accord with your working style. For instance, set week-to-week goals, such as getting a topic and doing some research the first week, finding a thesis by the second, more research the third week, an outline by the fourth week, finishing research by the fifth, writing a certain number of pages by the sixth, etcetera. Of course, there is usually less time than that, and many people don't start big papers until well into the semester, so daily goals work just as well.

—Casey China, Brown University, psychology
major

Give yourself plenty of time. I have a friend who does great work under pressure. Personally, I can't. However, I always told her that if she does so well when she has no time, think of what she could do if she really spent some time on it. We all get busy and it's hard to get everything done, but the sooner you start, the sooner you finish. And you'll have time to polish it up before you turn it in.

—Susan Reynolds, University of North
Carolina—Chapel Hill, American studies
major/art history minor

The best strategy for writing college papers is to start them *early*. Even if I just create a document on my computer desktop a couple of weeks or ten days ahead, it gets me thinking about the assignment that I will be writing. At this time, I try to jot down a few sentences or even the first paragraph, and a rough outline of ideas. Then, as the days go by before the paper is due, I fill in the blanks, writing a paragraph or two at a time. I find this gradual process lets me write a better-thought-out and clear paper. I am continually writing some, setting it aside, and then returning later to revise and write more. Best of all, I avoid last-minute mania and those painful all-nighters.

—Karen Meteyer, student writing assistant
at Dartmouth University

You and this topic are going to be spending a lot of time together, so you want to be sure you get along well. Remember that time you decided to drive across the country with a "buddy" you wanted to kill about three days into the trip? No? Well neither do we, but you get the idea.

> I would not like students to get the idea that clear writing is something that can be grafted on to sloppy thinking. Clear writing comes after, or during, the process of clear thinking.
>
> —Roger Brockett, An Wang Professor of Electrical Engineering and Computer Science, Harvard University

Drawing a Blank

If nothing comes immediately to mind, think way back to the beginning of the semester. There's probably a particular reason you decided to take the course in the first place.

> One original perception outweighs any amount of processed research.
>
> —Roger Stoddard, Curator of Rare Books, Harvard College Library

> If you're having a hard time coming up with a good topic, gripe about it periodically. Sounds stupid, but it helps keep the subject bubbling away on a back burner, which means you may actually come up with something good.
>
> —Becky Cary, Princeton University, molecular biology major

Maybe you have an interest that you could turn into a decent paper topic. If the only reason you decided to take the course in the first place was because it only had one paper and no final, you're going to have to dig a bit deeper.

> Never, ever, write the story about a college student waking in either a fraternity or sorority house, or a shabby apartment, hung over or strung out, and recalling that he or she had unprotected sex the night before. Write no stories about freshman mixers or last year's high school dance; this injunction includes the one about the parental car that was borrowed without permission, as well as the

formicary: an ant hill

damage done to it before it was returned. Try not to pay homage to a parent for bailing you out when you were arrested for some combination of the elements referred to above. All stories about high school friends killed or wounded in vehicular accidents should be written only after the junior year. Make something up (and find out how true it is). Make us worry. Make us wonder. Make us want to read the rest.

—Frederick Busch, Fairchild Professor of
Literature, Colgate University

Check out the notes you've taken (you did go to lectures, didn't you?) and look for thought-provoking, paper-friendly themes. Find something you discussed in class that could be expanded into a paper. Or even ask your instructor or TA.

> It was the most I ever threw up, and it changed my life forever.
>
> —Closing statement of Homer J. Simpson's college application essay

Another good idea is to make sure you know exactly what criteria the professor is using to grade your paper. While we don't condone carefully tailoring your paper to pander to the lecturer, it is important to figure out what style your prof is looking for. Would he or she rather see a ton of research or a compilation of original thoughts? Knowing such basic criteria will give you a good idea of where you're headed.

All of this seems really obvious, but it's crucial and too often overlooked. If you start out writing the wrong kind of paper, you're going to finish the wrong kind of paper and (most likely) hand it in.

Classifying Your Topic

In the course of narrowing down your topic, you're also going to place your paper into one of two general categories: analytical or argumentative. An analytical paper takes facts and examples and uses them to analyze a subject, while an argumentative paper uses facts to try to convince the audience of a particular viewpoint. Deciding which type of paper you're writing will help you determine your purpose: If you know you're writing an argumentative paper, it's merely a matter of picking what it is that you want to argue about.

Let's look at the two in more detail.

An•a•lyze (v.t.) 1. Separate into its elements; determine the constituents of. 2. Examine critically.

In an analytical paper, the writer breaks down a topic to its constituents through the process of researching in order to gain a fundamental understanding of the topic. These constituents can then be shuffled and rearranged to present bits and pieces of the topic from the perspective of the writer.

An analytical paper begins with a question. For example: How do Bentham and Mill's philosophies compare? The question is then examined by researching information and ideas that have already been published on the subject. By reading and understanding the ideas of experts, you can draw your own conclusions.

Let's say you decide to analyze the trend of athletes running for political office. The body of the paper will be comprised of evidence from primary sources (say, Jesse "The Body" Ventura's acceptance speech) and secondary sources (the analysis of his speech by fellow wrestlers/politicos). Finally, you'd discuss your interpretations and give final remarks.

Ar•gue (v.t.) 1. State reasons for and against; discuss. 2. Maintain; seek to prove

Most papers in college are argumentative because professors are more interested in what you think about a former pro wrestler running for governor than a list of athlete/politicians you found in an encyclopedia. The idea of an argumentative paper is not merely to report on a book, but to give evidence that supports or discredits a book's themes and ideas. Your position—that the trend of pro wrestlers turning politicians is detrimental to this country's well-being—will become this paper's thesis (see below). Your paper's main goal is to convince a reader to agree with your thesis.

quidnunc: an inquisitive person; a gossip

An argumentative paper on the same topic might attempt to demonstrate that the United States would be greatly benefited by deporting all pro wrestlers to the Antarctic. This purpose would be outlined in the thesis sentence, most likely in the first paragraph of the paper. No longer is the paper just a discussion of the topic; it is now an *interpretation* of the topic. For the body of the paper, select the sources that support your interpretation, providing evidence for your thesis.

> [Argumentative writing] entails the student learning how to advance a position based on a form of evidence that others can examine (texts, historical events, numerical data) and leading them to a preferred conclusion based on that evidence. Does this normally depend on getting the story "right" as they would when writing a book report? Yes. Is it guided by personal opinion as more obviously personal statements are? Yes. But it combines both elements in a new and more persuasive structure that is guided by an argument. It is this which teaches and which is most difficult for students to learn. They either want to put into an essay everything they know about the subject or their personal opinions as such. It is my job to teach them how to use the data to advance a personal outlook without it ever appearing to be such. [The essay] can, thus, be judged based on the argument and the evidence adduced, rather than whether one agrees with the opinion or likes the author.
>
> —Barry Shain, Associate Professor of
> Political Science, Colgate University

Turn Your Topic into a Purpose or
It's Really Terrific to be More Specific

Let's say you've decided you want to write about the philosopher Jeremy Bentham. Now while Mr. Bentham may be a fine, upstanding individual, his name alone will not suffice for a topic. What aspect of the topic do you wish to discuss? What, exactly, is the purpose of writing your paper?

- To analyze Bentham's main philosophies?
- To convince the reader that Bentham philosophies are applicable to modern society?
- To compare Bentham with another philosopher like J. S. Mill?

Once you have a purpose, you need to figure out how that purpose will be accomplished in the course of your paper. What aspects of this topic can you discuss? Brainstorming is a fine technique to get the ideas flowing: Write down everything you can, anywhere. Jot down examples, thoughts, ideas (good or bad), scribble— anything to get the creative juices flowing. Ask your friends for help.

> Scribble. Scribble all over the place, on napkins, on your assignment sheet, in your notebook, on your roommate. Just write down anything you could imagine might be relevant to the topic of the paper, no matter how seemingly trivial or off-topic it might seem. I have been saved on a few occasions by perusing my scribbles.
>
> —Andrew Sawtelle, Brown University

The Goldilocks Test

Whether you're writing an argumentative or an analytical paper, you need to have a specific question in mind before you start researching. Make sure your question passes the Goldilocks test: You don't want a topic too large in scope or too small, but one that's just right.

First, is it too broad? If your question is, "what were Jeremy Bentham's philosophies?" you're going to have some problems when you start researching and realize that the man had more philosophies than your dorm room has empty beer cans. Narrow it down, but not too far. "Describe what went through Jeremy Bentham's head on the morning of March 2, 1802" is a touch too narrow. You want a question that's, well, just right.

Give your topic a little test run. Search for it in a library catalog or an Internet search engine. If you get 25,000 responses, guess what, bunky? It's too broad. If you get zip-zero, you'd better expand. For example, if you go to HotBot.com and search for "Jeremy Bentham," you get more than 1,000 hits. If you search for "Jeremy Bentham's thoughts on March 2, 1802," the search engine returns a single hit, which turns out not to be particularly relevant. (Hotbot.com and other search engines are discussed in the chapter on researching.)

piepowder: a travelling man, a wayfarer, an itinerant merchant or trader

Brainstorming is important because it frees you to write down all the ideas you have and not worry about them being stupid. I think that a key problem with the way that I used to write was that I never would brainstorm. I would try to write a paper from intro through conclusion. This would make more work for myself in the end because I wouldn't realize what I really wanted to write about until I was almost done. It's important to put all the brainstorming ideas down on paper; once I visualize, I can organize better.

—Ashley Brown, Dartmouth University

While a professor will enjoy a topic that differs from those in the other twenty papers he reads, a hypercreative topic doesn't guarantee a good grade. Theses that propose zany ideas that are of little relevance frustrate the professor. Your professor wants to read a paper that demonstrates an understanding of the material. It's great to be original; just don't go overboard.

If you have general guidelines about a subject area or topic, but are in search of a more specific area of concentration, a little background research is probably in order. After all, you can't know what aspect of a topic you're interested in if you don't know anything about the subject.

Scouting Out Your Topic

It's great to pick an unusual topic, like Jungian symbolism in the images on the back of a Kraft Macaroni and Cheese package—especially if it interests you. If nobody else has ever written on said topic, however, research will be either extraordinarily frustrating or just plain impossible. Don't discount the idea until you've done a thorough sweep of library resources, however. Just because there aren't any texts on the subject doesn't mean scientific or scholarly journals aren't overflowing with relevant articles.

To get an idea of how much is out there, search your library through a computer terminal or the Internet, depending on what's available. If your library has everything on the Internet, you can check out a variety of topics without ever leaving your room.

Considering the technology that students have available to them, research via Web-based libraries is the best way to obtain the best information. For instance, at my university we have a library home page for the school. This home page has a wide variety of "article access" search engines that give you thousands upon thousands of articles relating to almost anything. Thus, instead of spending hours in a library looking for books or magazines on the topic of your paper, Web-based library search engines give you access to scholarly journals that look good in your paper.

—Chad Stansberry, University of Colorado
at Boulder, communications major

If you have a good idea for something you'd like to write about Jeremy Bentham, but you can't come up with a specific purpose, look up the call numbers of relevant books and go give them a quick browse. Take a peek at neighboring books in the stacks. Anything nearby will most likely be on the same topic, but with a different slant or purpose. There's a good chance something in one of those books will bite you—something printed in the books, we mean—not the spider that's decided to make a nest inside a copy of *Principles and Morals*.

Scoping out the books on the shelves is always a good idea so you can see a bit more than just their titles. Glance through a couple possibilities, and see if you think you can stomach reading them for hours and hours. If just flipping through the book bores you, it might be a good idea to rethink your topic.

Don't invest an inordinate amount of time scouring through these books, however. Absorbing too much information before you've settled on a clear topic can be overwhelming and confusing. If skimming through the books doesn't produce a topic, talk to your professor about it.

Have a story, not a topic. Too many writers, whatever their age, pitch ideas based on unfocused interest rather than on an idea, person, or trend involving impact, meaning, motion, tension, and color.

—Abe Peck, Chair, Magazine Program,
Medill School of Journalism,
Northwestern University; Contributing
Editor, *Rolling Stone*.

funambulist: a tightrope walker or rope dancer

Preliminary research is also a good idea because it lets you get acquainted with a topic. You're going to be spending a lot of time with this topic, so you want to get good and friendly. Think of it as a date. Sure, you can take your topic out for a nice, romantic dinner, but if the evening ends with a mere handshake, something's just not clicking. Make sure you and your topic are suitable for a long-term relationship. If you're not compatible, you want to break it off as soon as possible—the longer you continue with the same topic, the messier the breakup will be. Remember, there's no such thing as a prenuptial agreement between you and your research paper.

THESIS STATEMENT

> Developing a thesis is the most important part of prewriting. When writers are in a hurry, they often take shortcuts on this step. Starting to write a paper without a solid thesis will not save you time: When you are halfway through the paper at 1 A.M. and discover that you need to change your thesis and scrap much of what you have already hastily written, you will realize the value of spending an extra few minutes brainstorming about the thesis in the prewriting stage.
>
> —Kerry Flannery-Reilly, Princeton University

So you have a topic, you've narrowed it down or expanded it, and you're just itching to bury yourself in the library. Sorry, it's not quite time yet. You're close, but close counts only in horseshoes and hand grenades. If you don't want to be wandering around the library with a dazed look on your face, you need to solidify a thesis statement first. If you *do* want to be wandering around with a dazed look on your face, you might need a different kind of self-help book.

> One problem is finding not just a topic, but an original thesis. This is (again) a matter of reading, which students have not been trained to do, or at least not very well. What I tell students to do is write about a question that intrigues them and to mine the text for "answers," making lists of examples and passages.
>
> —Jane Chance, Professor of English, Rice University

Thesis statements are the cornerstone of any argumentative essay; if you're writing an analytical paper you really just need to have a solid question to ponder. (See above for more distinctions between the two.)

> This thesis provides a clear blueprint for the rest of the essay.
> —Tony Spanakos, Professor of Political
> Science, Tufts University

Your thesis will probably be one to two sentences, clearly and succinctly stating the purpose of your paper. In high school, your English teacher might have made you include with your thesis an explicit list of each of the points that would support your purpose. ("This viewpoint is supported by point one, point two, and point three.") That's most likely not necessary for your paper. You'll probably be going far beyond the old five-paragraph theme; listing every point just isn't practical.

Remember to actually stake out a position in your thesis, a position that can be defended and attacked. Go out on a limb here. If your thesis is something lame like, "Kraft macaroni is the cheesiest," it's going to be nearly impossible to make an intelligent argument. Just a sidenote—"cheesiest" is probably a word that should never appear in an academic paper of any sort.

> Trust your ideas and opinions. Do not be afraid to lock horns with
> an author, no matter how world-renowned that author may be. Your
> engagement will be more often than not generously rewarded.
> —Paul A. Silverstein, Mellon Fellow in the
> Humanities, Barnard College

It's much better to come out of the blue with a thesis like, "Kraft macaroni is highly symbolic of much of the later works of Jeremy Bentham because . . . ," and then scramble for evidence. Hopefully, you've done your preliminary research and realize that such a thesis is a doomed undertaking. Common sense should dictate whether you will be able to prove such a thesis.

syzygy: a conjunction or opposition, especially of the moon with the sun

The trick is to utilize the models and forms that are out there in ways that foster individual expression and creativity while nevertheless doing what papers are supposed to do: communicate and persuade.

—John Bendix, Professor of Women's
Studies, University of Pennsylvania

The most important thing to remember about your thesis is that this statement is the very heart of your essay. Everything you write from here on in must relate to the thesis statement, so it needs to be very clear and direct. If you're mushy and unclear with the thesis, the rest of your paper will follow in form.

[The thesis] helps me focus. I've had professors tell me they don't really care that much what you're writing as long as it's organized, and the thesis helps to organize the paper.

—Amanda Treyz, Brown University,
American civilization major

The thesis or question you come up with now isn't carved into a block of granite (unless your computer is really behind the times). It's quite probable that you'll want to change or modify it once you get farther along. Still, it's a good idea to have a definite purpose in mind before you hit the books, or valuable time will be wasted. Time that could be spent on more important things, like doing your laundry and playing video games.

Chapter Two

RESEARCHING

You're off to a good start. First of all, *you started*. You pondered the assignment, and scouted out a topic. Armed with your thesis and a sharp No. 2 pencil, you're now well enough equipped to hit the books.

> The only way that I actually get research and writing done is if I go somewhere quiet away from my roommates! When I work at home, I inevitably end up talking to my roommates, cleaning my room, and just generally procrastinating. When I need to work efficiently, I find that going to the library or computer center is most effective.
>
> —Lauren Margulies, Amherst College, history major

Just as there's no one type of paper, there's no one way to go about researching. With the ubiquity of computers in libraries and universities, methods and approaches to researching are continually changing and improving. The possibilities can be confusing, and certainly a little daunting.

You can find an overwhelming amount of information about any particular topic: the amount the U.S. government spent on toilet paper last year, the acid catalysts that are soluble in nonpolar organic solvents, the weather in Antarctica. Whether in textbooks, magazines, or journals; on the Internet, or in any of the numerous other media forms, finding resources is rarely the real problem. When so many resources are available, however, the main difficulty becomes trying to sort out the good from the bad, the worthwhile from the worthless.

The sources you find, wherever you find them, will provide the evidence and arguments for you to prove (or disprove) your thesis. The People in Charge of Such Things have classified sources into two categories: primary and secondary.

A primary source is straight from the horse's mouth. The text of a play you're analyzing is a primary source. An interview with an irate coal miner striking in the English mine that's described in your paper is also a primary source.

Secondary sources are a step away from the original sources. An expert commenting on the play you're analyzing is a secondary source. A labor union boss discussing an interview with a coal miner working in the strike you're examining is also a secondary source. By the way, Cliffs Notes™ are also secondary sources, but quoting from them will not score points with your professor.

Don't bother looking for tertiary or quaternary sources; they don't exist. No matter how many people are commenting on writings that discuss writings that analyze your play, it's still considered secondary.

Primary sources are probably going to be easier to come by for the majority of papers you'll write during your undergraduate career. If you're writing about a play, novel, or political treatise, odds are the professor thoughtfully had you purchase a copy (or two, if your professor wrote it himself) at the beginning of the semester. Owning copies of the books is nice anyway—you can scribble randomly, highlight profusely, and spill coffee guiltlessly.

Remember, you don't need to reread primary sources in their entirety. Assuming you read them the first time like you were supposed to (maybe if you didn't watch *Who Wants to Be a Millionaire* so much), just skim through looking for examples that support your thesis. Things that contradict your thesis are good too; addressing opposing arguments shows the professor that you've thoroughly considered the question.

Secondary sources may require a little more legwork. Finding good sources in your school library can be like a scavenger hunt, especially when you're in a large lecture and everyone's fighting for the same books. We here at the *Yale Daily News*

cacography: bad handwriting or bad spelling

are pacifists, but if it comes down to you, a classmate, and one ideal source . . . well, let's just say we won't be the ones to blame you for a few flagrant elbows.

Searching a library has only grown easier since the dawn of time (by the way, sweeping generalizations like *since the dawn of time* or *history has shown* annoy professors; never use them). It couldn't have been fun for the primitive cavemen to scavenge through all those rocks looking for the ideal piece of quartz. Today, there are computers that can do that for you.

FINDING STUFF IN THE LIBRARY
(or, Trying Not to Crack in the Stacks)

Most libraries follow the notorious Dewey Decimal System. Do you want to know who Dewey was? 'Course you do.

Melvil Dewey (1851–1931) Dewey attended Amherst College, where he later became a successful librarian, despite having the unfortunate name Melvil. His now notorious library classification system was described in a book he published in 1876. Dewey's other contributions towards the library sciences include being a founding member of the American Library Association and editing *Library Journal*.

> **Here are the basic categories:**
> 000 General Works
> 100 Philosophy and Psychology
> 200 Religion
> 300 Social Sciences
> 400 Languages
> 500 Natural Sciences and Mathematics
> 600 Technology and Applied Sciences
> 700 Fine Arts
> 800 Literature
> 900 Geography and History

Everything is then subdivided, so you don't have to search through thousands of books to find the ones you want. Other libraries don't always use this system, though, because that would be too easy. The Library of Congress has its own little classification, and the Yale University Library thinks it's so cool that it also created its own.

Top-20 U.S. College and University Libraries Based on Number of Volumes in Library, 1997

Source: Association of Research Libraries

Academic Institution	Volumes	Microforms
Harvard U.	13,617,133	8,146,817
Yale U.	9,932,080	6,475,762
U. of Illinois, Urbana	9,024,298	4,749,496
U. of California, Berkeley	8,628,028	5,798,420
U. of Texas	7,495,275	5,351,849
U. of California, Los Angeles	7,010,234	5,871,355
U. of Michigan	6,973,162	5,643,000
Columbia U.	6,905,609	5,217,558
Stanford U.	6,865,158	4,972,783
U. of Chicago U.	6,116,978	2,356,427
Cornell U.	6,113,346	7,164,967
Indiana U.	5,916,992	3,981,111
U. of Wisconsin	5,824,639	4,395,889
U. of Washington	5,715,202	6,526,689
Princeton U.	5,516,141	4,479,269
U. of Minnesota	5,490,668	5,391,112
Ohio State U.	5,087,336	4,364,755
U. of North Carolina	4,819,186	4,189,938
Duke U.	4,645,050	3,381,313
U. of Pennsylvania	4,546,667	3,155,776

panjandrum: a mock title for a person, real or imaginary, who has or claims to have great influence or authority

Classification systems are terrific once you know a book's number, but aren't terribly helpful otherwise. So, without further ado . . .

Finding the Sources You Want

Let's start off by saying that yes, libraries still have card catalogs. Card catalogs are terribly useful when the library's power is off or the computers have nasty viruses. Otherwise, they're really only helpful when you're searching for some terribly esoteric book that hasn't been read since 1925. Still, if all of a library's collection isn't in the computer system, the card catalog will prove invaluable.

> Almost all university libraries now have a paper catalogue with older holdings and an electronic catalogue with newer holdings. Do not limit your research to the electronic catalogue. A lot of interesting things were written (and acquired by libraries) before the mid-1970s.
>
> —Leora Auslander, Professor of History,
> University of Chicago

Assuming you're looking for something more plebeian, a computerized catalog should be much more useful. Search by subject and enter keywords from the handy thesis you've concocted. If the system comes up with too many hits, or worse, too many irrelevant hits, you can narrow the field using Boolean operators. What are Boolean operators? Glad you asked.

How to Search (Boolean Searching)

George Boole (1815–64), was an English mathematician who pioneered the field of symbolic logic. The Boolean operators, named in his honor, include AND (looking for all terms), OR (looking for at least one), and NOT (to exclude a term). They're always referred to in capital letters, but you don't have to type them that way. So if your keyword search for "Kraft" brings up too many books about their disgusting Velveeta products instead of their fine macaroni and cheese, try searching for "Kraft AND macaroni" or "Kraft NOT Velveeta." Some search engines also allow you to use NEAR to specify that you want to find two terms close to each other within the article.

If your keyword searches bring up the names of primary sources, try typing those into a Title search. Often you can find an anthology of the primary source with criticisms all-in-one. Jot down the call numbers of everything vaguely relevant and go take a peek on the shelves. Similar books whose titles didn't come up in your search will be shelved right next to the ones the computer found for you. If that's still not enough literary goodness for you, check out the bibliography in an especially relevant book for any other helpful sources.

It's possible you've typed every combination of words into the computer terminals, but nothing's coming up. Instead of sitting there and typing insults and curses (the computers don't understand you anyway), try a different route.

A Different Route

The trail of journals, magazines, microfilm/fiche, and books is endless. Don't get discouraged when your search comes up empty. We'll throw out a few tips we think are particularly valuable, but this list isn't comprehensive by any means. Have a chat with your friendly librarian (most of them don't bite) and see what he or she suggests.

Periodicals (Magazines and Journals)

If you're looking for information on a particularly timely topic, journals might just be the way to go. They'll most likely have very up-to-date information and shouldn't be any harder to search through than book collections. Journals are also fun because they're targeted very specifically. Check out *Pediatric Pharmacotherapy* or the ever-popular *Journal of Buddhist Ethics* to find in-depth info on arcane subjects.

Encyclopedias, Dictionaries, Fact Books, Atlases

The entries in encyclopedias are probably not detailed enough to make them valuable sources. However, don't overlook them if you're working on a topic about which you are less than informed. An encyclopedia's value lies in its brevity and clarity—attributes that can help you gain a basic understanding of a topic before opening more in-depth, and probably more confusing, works.

bissextile: pertaining to February 29th

FINDING STUFF ON THE INTERNET
(or There's No Reason to Whine about Searching Online)

> One tendency I have noticed among students, both undergraduate and graduate, is an inability to use electronic media when they are carrying out research. Our administrators and some teachers think that students are somehow able to do electronic research just because they play computer games. That is clearly not the case; as someone who played computer games twenty years ago, I know that they contributed nothing to my ability to understand scholarly research by means of computers. In a way, the challenges of research have not changed over the past twenty years: Students still need to figure out which reference works or databases are most appropriate for which kinds of classes and assignments. Now, however, they are confronted with many more ways of seeking information, which can make the search for scholarly sources much more complicated.
>
> —Peter Caldwell, Associate Professor of History, Rice University

Anyone can post information on the Internet. This is both a blessing and a curse. On the one hand, finding Web pages devoted to a particular topic, no matter how arcane, is rarely difficult. On the other hand, finding a page with validated, accurate information that you can use in an academic paper is rather tougher. Sure, Lamar Higgins from Peach Tree, Nebraska may be "99.9 percent sure" about his interpretation of *Hamlet*, but will your professor be impressed when you cite "The Personal Home Page of Lamar Higgins" in your bibliography?

There isn't a whole lot of help out there to help you evaluate the pages you find on the Internet. Your best defense is to make sure everything you take from the Internet is well documented, so anyone else can find the same information. First, find the author of the page. Informational Web pages are often authored by organizations or corporations rather than individuals. If the page was created by a respectable organization, its information will be more trustworthy than that from a page whose author is anonymous. Look for documentation for each piece of information provided on the page: Just as you're being responsible by documenting your resources, any good Web page should do the same.

Best Web Sites to Waste Time

1. www.treeloot.com—The undisputed champion. Win thousands of dollars just by clicking the right spot on the tree. Be prepared to waste entire weeks.
2. www.go2net.com/useless—The Useless Pages. The best collection of utter wastes of time on the Internet.
3. www.freelotto.com—The chance to win a million dollars every day? We're there.
4. www.allmusic.com—Read about the history of a band you've never heard of, then follow the links to learn about the solo album the bass player recorded along with the lead singer of a now-defunct band you've also never heard of. Good times are had by all.
5. www.jeopardy.com—Play the online game! Compete against thousands of other college students who also can't find anything to do!
6. www.napster.com—Download the software so you can find endless MP3s, single-handedly use half your university's band width, get sued by Metallica, and never do work again.

Just because the information on the Web is often unreliable doesn't mean the Internet isn't a valuable resource. Locating government information, statistics, experts, and people to contact takes less time than it

> Ooh, they have the Internet on computers now!
>
> —Homer J. Simpson

takes for a twelve-cent goldfish to kick the bucket. Many libraries now have their electronic catalogs available over the Net so you can search them without leaving your university-prohibited rice cooker unattended. Journals, too, are listed— many in convenient, electronic forms. Remember, however, that the Internet shouldn't be your only source. Using books and journals not only supplements and guides your Internet search, but it also serves as a check against fraudulent Internet information. If a respectable published journal claims that "penguins are our Antarctic friends" but an Internet page proclaims that "penguins are the most violent creatures ever to waddle the face of this planet," you'll know that the Internet information is faulty.

hylomania: love of wood

Where to Go: Better Bets on the Internet

New York Times "CyberTimes Navigator"
(www.nytimes.com/library/tech/reference/cynavi.html)

The homepage used by the *New York Times* newsroom—a motley collection of links, from search engines to government records to reference desk pages.

Bartleby's Quotations
(www.bartleby.com)

Convenient searches by subject, turns up great numbers of results.

Whatis.com
(www.whatis.com)

Answers all of your technological questions. Defines computer-related terms from *abacus* to *Z39.50* (a protocol used to search for bibliographic information).

The WWW Virtual Library
(www.vlib.org)

Links to pages about everything you can think of. Even beer-brewing.

CIA World Fact Book
(www.odci.gov/cia/publications/factbook/index.html)

The CIA's lowdown on every country in the entire world.

Search Engines

There's a lot of junk out there, and an ever-increasing number of ways for you to search for it. Remember, these search engines all employ our good friends, the Boolean operators (see above). A quick look at the best search dot coms:

1. **HotBot**—Provides the most useful, accurate results thanks to a new technology it calls Direct Hit. Direct Hit tracks which results users click and how long the users stay at each site, then ranks them accordingly. HotBot doesn't let you fine-tune your search as much as some other engines, but its results are clearly the best of the bunch.

2. **Excite**—Has the second best search accuracy, behind HotBot. Although the searches aren't as precise, it does have a lot of fun extras, like e-mail and news headlines. It also brings up a list of relevant terms it thinks you'd like.

3. **AltaVista**—AltaVista is mediocre at searching. It does, however, claim to have the largest index of Web sites on the Internet, letting you click through by category. Many of the sites links are dead, however, meaning that the pages they link to are no longer functional. On the other hand, AltaVista is extremely easy to use, so it's a great site for beginners.

4. **Infoseek**—Crappy accuracy, but it's easy to use. It also packs goodies like free e-mail, a personal start page, shopping, and the all-important smut filter.

5. **Lycos**—The worst accuracy of any, but really easy searching. Has e-mail, directories. Use it only if you like the idea of only typing the five letters of its name instead of the six it takes to type "hotbot."

Some sites, called metasearchers, let you search multiple engines all at the same time. The best of these are SavvySearch and MetaCrawler, and they're definitely worth your time. Ask Jeeves is also fun and easy, if not quite as helpful.

Plagiarism (or Copy and Paste Blows Up in Your Face)

It's important to remember that, while the aforementioned resources can make the collection of information easier than ever, their convenience is a double-edged sword. Copying and pasting paragraphs from the Internet leads to one of the most common and most perilous pitfalls of writing—plagiarism. Professor Christopher Weare from the Annenberg School for Communication at the University of Southern California, warns, "The Internet has made cut and paste 'borrowing' so easy that many students are knowingly and unknowingly plagiarizing all the time."

coprolite: petrified reptile dung

Notes you take from the Internet need to be treated just like any other information you find during the course of your research. Documenting Internet sources can be tricky, especially since a lot of the old handbooks on documentation were written before the Web became such a phenomenon. For good information on documentation, check these Web pages:

- http://www.dartmouth.edu/~sources/
- http://www.lycoming.edu/dept/library/internet/citeweb.htm
- http://www.uvm.edu/~ncrane/estyles/

So what is plagiarism, exactly? We're glad you asked.

Pla•gia•rism (n.) The offering of another's artistic or literary work as one's own

When you use someone else's words or ideas without citing them, you're plagiarizing. It's like when Minni Vanilli got up there on stage and sang along with music someone else had recorded, earning tons of cash and a Grammy Award, only to have it all stripped away and end up getting laughed out of the business.

Plagiarism cannot be avoided by minor adjustments. Professor Jeannine Diller of Seattle Pacific University explains that, "If you paraphrase an author's words, substituting synonyms here and there and juggling the sentence order around, you are not saying anything which the author isn't saying."

Simply put, you can't pass off other people's writing or ideas as your own. A lot of the time plagiarism is involuntary—a few sentences or an idea from a source somehow makes it unchanged into the finished paper. Even inadvertent plagiarism can get you an F on that paper and, in the worst-case scenario, suspension or expulsion from school. It's just that wrong.

Anyone who's had some experience clicking around on the World Wide Web (see above) has probably run into the newest trend in blatant plagiarism: Web sites that allow you to purchase and download finished, graded papers. We know, you're curious. Go check them out, but don't even think about patronizing them.

There's the crowd-pleasing SchoolSucks.com, the ever-popular Cheater.com, and even PlanetPapers.com. Those are free and especially laughable. If you're willing to pay for their questionable services, there's The Paper Store and the prestigious-sounding Academic Research Group.

We've looked into these papers; we tried to find a paper to buy for the *Guide to Writing College Papers*. We've concluded that they enslave six-year-olds in sweat shops to write them. If you want a good laugh, by all means check out a free paper site. But trying to pass off these wastes of paper is an insult to your professor and to you. Even when it seems like your professor is horribly out of touch with the world, don't underestimate his ability to recognize a fraudulent paper when he sees it.

New sites on the Internet are also combating the ills of the term paper locales. Plagiarism.org and EVE can both scour the Internet and compare thousands of papers with your own to help your professor determine if you've been trying to cheat the system.

So here's the bottom line. Deep down we all know there's no real point in being in college if you're not trying to learn something. If you really think passing off somebody else's work as your own is the way to go, maybe college isn't really where you belong.

Interviewing

Don't underestimate the value of stepping out of the library and finding a real, live expert on a subject. Just because someone's not dead yet doesn't mean that he or she can't be a valuable source for your paper.

Books cannot always please, however good; minds are not ever craving for their food.

—George Crabbe (1754–1832)

cribellate: of spiders that produce multiple strands of entangling silk

How do you find someone who knows stuff about your topic?

> Use your classmates, professor, roommates, anyone. You may live with an expert on your subject and not even know it. Everyone can offer a fresh perspective on a topic. Resources are not only in the library, and interviewing or just discussing the topic with someone can help you see more than one side. For example, I had a paper for my Southern Women's Lit class about a slave from Edenton, North Carolina. My roommate was from there, and she gave me pictures, brochures, and information on the town. It helped me write the paper, and my teacher was impressed with all the extras I brought in.
>
> —Susan Reynolds, University of North Carolina—Chapel Hill, American studies major/art history minor

Here's another interviewer's tip. Before you go into an interview, you want to make sure you're armed with enough ammunition. Prepare a number of questions ahead of time, so you don't blank out and waste both your and your interviewee's time.

PANIC MODE (or Where to Look When You Can't Find a Book)

Obviously, this chapter has been trying to tell you how to get your research done *responsibly*. You don't really need to buy a book to learn how to slack off and cut corners. Nevertheless, no one expects that anyone will always start a paper three weeks before it's due.

> Procrastination is admirable; it means that you are taking advantage of all that life has to offer without dwelling on the minor details, like term papers. But when crunch time comes, you have to act fast.
>
> —Brad Olson, Harvard, government major

So you waited until the last minute, and now all of the relevant books are checked out of your college library, probably by all the responsible students in your class who did their research when they were supposed to. First off, remember to check other libraries too. Your town or city probably has a public library, and while it may not seem prestigious enough for a great academic like you, it probably has a decent collection of books.

Remember to check for anthologies. These are like journals, but in book form, often containing analysis by experts as well as primary texts. Just because the whole book isn't on your subject doesn't mean you should overlook it.

If all the books on a topic are checked out of the library, the idea's probably not too original. If you can come up with a unique topic, it'll be easier to find resources, you can be more creative with your writing, and your professor will probably enjoy it too.

Your best option? Don't put off doing the research next time.

> Students consider research of any kind as extra work, "one more thing to do," and often avoid it at all costs. This includes computer-assisted reporting, library research, courthouse document reviews, reading old newspapers, even reading today's newspaper. Telling students that this kind of research will make their writing assignment better, help them get better grades, and help them prepare for a job as a journalist often seems to fall on deaf ears. It is hard to sell students on doing "one more thing" when many students have a maximum load of classes, jobs on the side, or just can't understand the value of such work.
>
> —Michael F. Lane, Assistant Professor,
> Department of Journalism and Public
> Information, Emerson College

NOTE TAKING (or Forty-Five Cents'll Get You a Nice Pencil)

No single note-taking strategy applies to every student. No note-taking strategy applies to every subject. While we wouldn't presume to tell you *the* way to take notes, we will try to give you some pointers and some tactics that other students use.

ulotrichous: woolly haired

When I was in high school my teachers taught me a valuable lesson about writing research papers: note cards. At the time I didn't recognize the value of this technique, but I use it whenever I write a research paper. The technique is simple, but efficient. When reading a source I always have a stack of note cards on hand to copy a relevant quote or piece of information relating to my paper. After I finish my research, I divide the cards into sections according to sections of my paper, then proceed to make an outline. It seems like a lengthy process, but it's a great way to organize a paper. I admit it takes some planning, and you can't use this technique the night before a paper is due, but it is a great way to keep everything organized.

—Anne Stancil, Davidson College, senior,
English major

Other students, however, prefer their own note-taking methods:

I find that index cards are cumbersome and useless, and it is easy to lose one or for them to get out of order.

—Stephanie Obodda, Princeton University

I generally take notes on my sources, and using these notes, I write my paper directly onto the computer. I can't be bothered with outlines or notecards, which seem pointless, probably because we were often forced to do them in high school.

—Katia Fredriksen, Princeton,
psychology major

Note-taking methods are up to you. You can use notecards, loose-leaf paper, or type your notes straight onto the computer. Write with bulleted fragments or complete sentences. Some students get eccentric by stretching out butcher paper and writing random facts in random order. Others type ideas into their laptops. Still others write facts on Post-it® Notes and organize them on their walls.

I first write down any ideas that I think are important with page numbers for applicable references. From these detailed notes, which are usually a page or two long, I jot down my basic ideas for organization. Usually, I have a phrase or two for each point, followed by a few notes about details. Even though this outline is no more than a few lines, I have a definite idea of how I want to present my argument before I begin my paper.

—Carrie Arthur, Davidson College,
English major

I often create computer files for each new element of information and all its subsequent parts. I also create files for each person I've interviewed and include in the file all other pieces of information that relate to that person or what that person has to say. Then, before writing, I print out all the files and organize them into an outline. This keeps information handy and ready for incorporation into copy. This sounds simple, and really it is, but you'd be surprised how many folks don't do this essential step. There was a time when I didn't really organize very well and it showed in my writing, which was not as meticulous as it should have been considering the wealth of information that I gathered. This is actually an organizational tip that I got from Pulitzer Prize–winning journalist Russell Carollo. Very effective.

—Jordan Smith, freelance writer, master's
candidate in journalism at University of
Texas—Austin

Highlighting, underlining, and scribbling in the margins can be fun for a while, but once the novelty of writing in your books wears off, make sure you jot down some actual notes on index cards or loose-leaf paper or whatever you're using. The whole point of note taking is to collect all the pertinent ideas in one place, not to have to rummage back through an entire book for them.

Students often have a difficult time presenting coherent accounts of the arguments of others. This is especially true if different writers adopt different approaches to their subject. Careful reading must precede careful writing.

—Murray Dry, Professor of Law,
Middlebury College

oneirocritic: someone who interprets dreams

Read *for* your thesis. Don't just read through a document and take random notes; you'll get bogged down with irrelevant information. Instead, you should constantly consider whether a fact, idea, or quote applies to your thesis. If you're not sure that it relates, keep it. It's much easier to get stuck with extra notes than it is to come back to the library and look for more.

Keep your notes succinct and to the point, but don't leave out anything. Don't think you'll remember a point later—we know you have a lot on your mind. Write it down.

If you have to read without knowing your specific purpose, just make sure you highlight and underline and make little notes in the margin to remind you where certain ideas are. The more easily identifiable your scratches in your book are, the easier it will be to locate supporting evidence or quotes as you begin to outline your paper.

Try to write legibly. You'll thank yourself later.

Rather than writing bibliographic information on all of your notecards, come up with a key to quickly associate which note came from which source. Try color-coding or numbering. For an added challenge, affiliate each source with one of the United States, then label each notecard with the state flower, tree, song, etcetera. Actually, we take it back. That's probably not such a good idea.

> Of course I usually need to incorporate facts, examples, or quotes in my academic writing. In order to tackle this often overwhelming task, I first make a general outline, noting the general structure of my impending nightmare, breaking it down into more manageable, less daunting steps. Next, I go through my sources and mark the places from which I may use information. The more sophisticated and clear this process, the easier it is when I need to plug in everything. Sometimes I will color code topics or themes. Other times I'll keep a master list by theme or subject with sources and page numbers. This way, when it comes time to write each section, I know exactly where to look, rather than needing to frantically search through all of the books, journals, articles, and notes strewn across my room.
>
> —Samantha Coren Spitzer, Brown
> University, sociology major

Put the page number where you found the information after each and every note.

Keep ideas or conclusions of your own in a separate section. If you're reading through a book and suddenly have a great insight of your own, write your thoughts on a separate card. That way you'll be sure to know later which thoughts are your own and which are your sources.

Photocopying only delays the inevitable. It may seem like a good idea to copy a page out of a book or journal, but you're still going to have to take notes on it at some point. You might as well do it in the library where it's quiet. Incidentally, trying to translate a photocopied source into a paper without first taking notes is a bad idea. The note-taking step is essential because it forces you to read the source, evaluate it, and put in into your own words. Without notes, you're more likely to plagiarize, intentionally or not.

> Don't wait until you have all your research to start writing. If you start your paper, and see what direction it begins to take, then you will know more about what you need to research. If you gather all your sources, and then start, chances are you won't know where to start and your paper will not be as focused as it should be.
>
> —Susan Reynolds, University of North Carolina—Chapel Hill, American studies major/art history minor

If two of your sources say the same thing, that's great. You can use agreeing viewpoints to back each other up. Likewise, if two sources contradict each other, make a note of that too. The more sides to an issue you can present, the more obvious it will be to your professor that you understand what you're writing about and that you've conducted thorough research.

Make sure to use a good variety of sources. Sure, you might find one book that just has everything you need, but just think how sad your bibliography is going to look with that one little citation all alone. At the same time, let's not go overboard. Putting down twenty-five different sources for a six-page paper might look impressive, but your professor knows full well that you're just trying to pad your stats.

tatterdemalion: a tattered or ragged person

Take Note

As a student and scholar, I find that the most effective way to write good papers is to do two things before the writing begins: Read the text carefully and thoroughly, taking extensive notes. I underline a lot in the text and also take separate notes on the readings, often copying important points from the text into my notebook. This may be done on computer, but I find that actually writing notes out by hand gives you more time to think about the material and impress it upon your mind.

—Linda Angst, Professor of Sociology and
Anthropology, Earlham College

Take specific notes on what you have read, and from those notes many words and phrases will resonate not only with what you want to say but with how to say it. Read an assignment more than once. This will deepen your appreciation of arguments and ideas. Writing is the aftermath of knowing what you think. Improving writing requires practicing simple exercises such as taking notes and rereading. Our anorexic culture insists on less for mind and body. This can never be good for writing.

—Jonathan Imber, Professor in Ethics,
Wellesley College

Many students take very sparse notes in class and on readings—and quite incoherent ones to boot. When asked why, they often answer that they can remember most ideas without jotting them down and may need only a one-word cue later on to recall those that don't stick. Multifaceted research shows neither of these beliefs credible. It also advises that notes not be taken for "remembering points later on." The act of selectively writing ideas down as we hear them, looking at them being written on the page and so forth, is key to how ideas are encoded and stored in memory in the first place. It is key also to how well they can be retrieved. Using several sensory and cognitive modalities in the process, placing ideas in rich verbal contexts (a cognitive process called "elaboration") is key to useful and coherent recall. It also promotes learning while it is happening. Selectively organizing ideas we hear in coherent notes involves identifying their significance. It often involves tracing out certain of their implications and relations to other ideas. Good notes form key components of the course papers or test answers students are asked to generate later on.

—Bill Puka, Professor of Philosophy and
Psychology, Rensselaer Polytechnical
Institute

As you go, make a working bibliography. Write down all the important information on each book you use: author, title, editor, edition number, publisher, city of publication, year of publication, issue number, volume, page numbers, height, weight, eye color, and anything else you might need. Jotting down the call numbers isn't such a bad idea either, in case you need to find a source again later. Overlooking this step now can lead to potential plagiarism problems down the road, so don't take it too lightly.

> While you're researching and gathering resources, it is handy to keep index cards with all the bibliographic information for a source on each card, or to keep a running list of sources. This helps SO MUCH when you're doing end notes, footnotes, parenthetical notes, and/or bibliographies. Sometimes you might put a good quote or specific topic on the index card. Using index cards with topics and with specific references can be a great visual aid for organizing your paper and writing the outline.
>
> —Casey China, Brown University,
> psychology major

Avoiding Plagiarism (Again)

It's so important that we had to include two sections on it. The note-taking step is where most involuntary plagiarism occurs, so it's a good idea to consider how to avoid it.

If you give credit in your paper for any ideas, words, or other constructions that you have borrowed from other places, you're not plagiarizing. That includes anything you use from magazines, movies, Web pages, advertisements, songs, pamphlets, TV shows, and any other resources you use. Whether it's just an idea or an exact phrase, document it. Similarly, give credit for any diagrams or pictures that you don't create yourself.

To make sure you can accomplish this in your paper, make sure to paraphrase instead of copying when you take notes. Sure, you'll need the occasional exact quote to spice up your paper, so if you see a good juicy one, go ahead and copy

titubation: a staggering or unsteadiness of walk or posture

it down. Make sure you use quotation marks so it's obvious that it's a quotation. Really obvious—maybe you want to highlight it or circle it so you'll be sure to recognize it later as someone else's words. But for the most part, make sure to put what you read into your own words right into your notes. If you copy down something verbatim, there's a very good chance you won't remember it's a quote later when you finally get around to the draft.

Paraphrasing is basically putting ideas you read into your own words. Although using direct quotes may be easier, paraphrasing looks and flows better in your paper. Paraphrased ideas allow you to write a paragraph in your own words, using other people's ideas (as long as you attribute them properly). Direct quotes are nice occasionally to add flavoring, but they tend to disrupt the flow of your writing when used too frequently.

Don't paraphrase something if you don't understand it. If you find an incredibly convoluted paragraph in a scholarly text (imagine that!), and you're not sure if you've interpreted it correctly, be safe and don't use it for your paper. The following sentence, for example, is probably not prime material for paraphrasing.

"The banal, exuberantly American macaroni-centric ethos permeating the nation is underscored by a profound and fundamental abhorrence of all things de frommage," writes our fictional, and very unclear, Professor Lamar Higgins.

If you paraphrase incorrectly, you're basically going to be attributing an incorrect idea to the author. And if the author happens to be someone your professor knows (you'd never believe how many authors your professors know—they went to high school with at least twenty of them), your prof will be upset. "But Professor Higgins *hates* macaroni," your professor will say.

Any particular facts you get from a source need to be documented. If you read in a book that Kraft Macaroni and Cheese is 65.4 percent cheesier than the leading brand, you need to say where you found that fact. However, you don't have to worry about documenting generalities. A sentence like, "Macaroni and cheese is a popular dinner for Americans of all ages," requires no attribution.

Chapter Two

Opinions naturally need to be credited to those who hold them. If Professor Lamar Higgins of the University of Peach Tree has a change of heart and writes in his book that he believes Kraft Macaroni and Cheese to be the cheesiest, you better be sure to say where he wrote that. Otherwise you could be in some big trouble, mister.

baldersnatch: an ugly mythical monster

ORGANIZING YOUR PAPER

Let's recap. At this stage in the game, you've got your thesis, stating your paper's purpose, and your research notes, supporting, defending, or providing background information about your thesis. Considering the prewriting stage completed, a hasty college student might jump headfirst into draft writing at this point. But not you. No, you've come this far responsibly, so you might as well finish things responsibly.

We talked to a lot of professors (the people who grade your papers) during the course of writing this book, and a great number of them discussed the vital importance of organization in a paper. J. David Parker, a history professor at Washington and Lee at Madison, explains it succinctly: "When preparing an essay, begin by **organizing your evidence**." Other professors agree that organizing is important.

> Good writing rarely happens all at once. It requires disciplined work. Once you have researched your subject and are ready to write your first sentence, don't. Instead, spend your first work session organizing your material into an outline. Then work in phases to flesh your draft out from bullets to sentences to whole text. At last, let the draft cool before you proofread and proofread, again.
>
> —Frank Durham, Professor of Journalism,
> University of Texas—Austin

Get Organized

It's been my experience that many students underestimate the significance of writerly organization—from the use of invention techniques, such as brainstorming, in order to generate ideas to the drafting of an outline, however brief, in order to keep oneself on track—when starting to write. As much as we like to believe that writing is an "inspiration" that suddenly strikes us, akin to lightning, such inspiration is more the product of good preparation than anything else. This applies both to in-class essays or exams as well as those composed outside of class.

—Stephen M. Byars, Associate Director of the Writing Program, University of Southern California

In real estate, three factors determine the value of a property—location, location, and location. A similar truth applies to any type of writing. Its value is determined by organization, organization, and organization. A good essay always starts out with a clear statement of what its thesis or argument will be, previews how the rest of the essay will support and prove the thesis, and concludes with a reminder of what it has accomplished.

—Thomas Hamm, Archivist and Professor of History, Earlham College

If you can nail down the outline of your paper, the actual writing process will be a cinch. Having all your main points organized first allows you to go back and worry only about filling in the specifics from your index cards. It's easy. If you don't outline before you write, it's going to take a lot longer to write.

Seeing your thoughts laid out in front of you will also show you where the gaps or problems are, allowing you to fix them before the paper gets too far along (more specifically, before it's five in the morning on the day your paper's due).

So, let's examine our options.

In this corner, from New Haven, Connecticut, weighing in at 175 pounds, we have a snappy, poignant paper that flows well and lays out its argument in a cohesive fashion! It's looking especially persuasive tonight, Rick.

bezoar: supposed antidote against poison

In the opposite corner, hailing from Cambridge, Massachusetts, and weighing in at a flabby 305 pounds, we have a wandering, confused paper lacking cohesiveness and direction that took the author twice as long to write. I don't know, Rick, it doesn't look like the challenger is ready for this fight. . . .

And the bell clangs, the fight is on. The two move into the ring. . . ouch, the challenger is on his back. . . this one is over! Oh, the humanity!

STARTING THE OUTLINE (or Plan Out What It's All About)

> The outline is one of the most valuable tools for writing, yet experienced writers often scoff at the outline as a technique for lesser writers. There is no substitute for a good outline. My uncle once told me that a tennis player is never too good to move his feet to get into position to return a volley. The same holds true for writing —a writer is never too good to write an outline.
>
> —Kerry Flannery-Reilly, Princeton University

You may already have a good idea of where your outline's headed. Well done. If not, don't panic. Go through your notes, and start sorting them by topic. If you used index cards, put them in little piles of related subjects (or build large piles, depending on how long you spent in the library). If all of your notes fall into a few distinct piles, you've just found a nice way to organize your paper. Make each of the piles into a division of your paper, and subdivide as suitable. If you're finding your notes divide less nicely into fifty-seven (or any odd number not divisible by pi) different topics, you may be examining them too narrowly. Look for broad trends and related ideas.

Now type or write up your divisions into some form of outline. Don't worry about where the Roman numerals go or whether you should be capitalizing or not. We're talking "outlining" in the organizational sense, not the anal, "lowercase letter, indent three times" sense. Use dashes, bullets, or whatever works for you.

If you can find only one supporting idea to go under a heading, you've found a weak area. Congratulations, Skippy. A little more research might be in order to flesh out that part of your paper, or you could consider dropping it altogether. Ignoring the weak area and hoping that your professor doesn't notice is also a possibility, just one that we don't recommend.

> I always compose an outline for any research or analytical paper I write. I make the first line my thesis, and then every point under that thesis statement represents a main point. I carefully write each point in grammatically parallel sentence form. Under each point, I list my supporting data and examples, with references if needed. Then, when it comes time to actually write the paper, I use each of the main points as the topic sentence for my paragraphs (since I've already carefully written each, this part is really easy). Each supporting detail then becomes a sentence or two within that paragraph (or sometimes even a subordinate paragraph itself). Also, since all the topic sentences are grammatically parallel, it's easy for the reader to recognize when I've moved onto another point.
>
> —Michael Kimberly, Princeton,
> chemistry major

CREATING AN ABSTRACT

If you're trying to avoid aimless writing, you've got to avoid aimless outlining first. Professor Glaser of Tufts University explains how aimless writing occurs:

> Oftentimes students make big choices in writing papers, choices that can be likened to a fork in the road when it becomes clear that we are lost. While it is best to go back to the fork in the road instead of continuing, very few people do. That is, most students continue writing papers that are going nowhere simply because they have not invested time and effort pursuing a particular strategy. This is never a good reason to continue and most often leads to a lousy outcome.
>
> —John Glaser, Associate Professor and
> Chair of the Department of Political
> Science, Tufts University

dactylonomy: the art of counting on the fingers

Some professors and students recommend that you summarize your main points to ensure that you understand where the paper is going.

> Over the last thirty years I have read thousands of social science essays by graduate and undergraduate students. The most pervasive problem I encounter is the student's inability to state succinctly the point or argument of the paper. Sometimes, the point will not be clear to the student until one or more drafts have been written. That's fine. But once it has become clear, the student should be able to state it in 100 words, and then redraft the paper so that the major point comes through loudly and clearly.
>
> I recommend the strategy of actually creating an abstract for each paper. This exercise focuses the mind; the exercise is especially revealing when it proves difficult to write the abstract. If the topic sentences, read sequentially, illustrate the thesis of the paper, chances are that you have at least a viable essay in your hands.
>
> —Howard Gardner, Professor of Education, Harvard University

ORGANIZING THE ARGUMENTATIVE PAPER

Argumentative papers, as we've discussed earlier, will probably be the ones you come across most often in college. Here are some tips and an example sketch to get you on the right track.

First, remember that you're arguing something. Thus, "argumentative." Still with us? Think of it literally—you're trying to win an argument, so each of your points needs to be a good one. Don't think you can sneak a weak fourth point in just because you had three big, juicy ones preceding it. If it's really pathetic, leave it out or expand on it.

Pretend you, the big hotshot lawyer, are making your case in front of a court:

"Point one: The defendant's fingerprints were on the doorknob." Good.

"Point two: The defendant's alibi for the night in question is more full of holes than a good Swiss cheese." Fine.

"Point three: The defendant looks like a guy I once knew who stole a bag of Skittles from the 7-11." Laughter from the jury.

Secondly, if you're trying to prove a point about, say, a novel you read for class, use as many examples as you can find to illustrate your point. Say you're writing about a character like the ever-popular Madame Defarge from *A Tale of Two Cities*, attempting to show how she's motivated by nastiness. Don't just give one example and think you're done. Instead, include several relevant examples in your outline: her snarling quotes, that shroud she keeps knitting, and her fondness for the guillotine. Give so many instances that it'll be difficult to believe that your character isn't one cold-hearted bastard.

Start with a nice introductory paragraph, setting the scene and working up to what the point of this paper will be. The point, of course, is clearly and succinctly presented in your good buddy, the thesis statement.

The body of the paper will consist of your supporting points and their discussions. Come up with a topic sentence for each of your points, and list all the notes you have that support this point. Give examples, and demonstrate how each of these examples is relevant. Go through each of your strong points in the same manner.

> Think of examples from the novel, play, or essay that support your thesis. Come up with two or three categories of examples. Take a blank sheet of paper and thumb through the book, writing down page numbers and short descriptions of the examples divided into the categories. This sheet will be incredibly helpful when you actually sit down to write the paper, and will also help you judge the viability of your thesis.
>
> —Kerry Flannery-Reilly, Princeton University

bloviate: to speak pompously

> The largest problem I confront when reading student papers is the lack of an argument cogently articulated and supported. Very often, I have received papers which are little more than summaries of the relevant readings with little original engagement with the ideas presented.
>
> —Paul A. Silverstein, Professor of
> Humanities, Barnard College

After going through all of your points, conclude. What have each of these points illustrated in relation to your topic? Discuss your thesis again. What does it all mean? Draw your own conclusions here. Show you can think for yourself.

ORGANIZING THE ANALYTICAL PAPER

Your approach to an analytical paper will be similar but without the need to persuasively argue a point. As before, set up the question that you're studying with background material, then give the question itself. Don't actually write a question, as this looks like a sixth grader's science project. Translate it into sentence form. Say something truly scientific sounding like "this paper will examine the effects of cheese and macaroni products on the palettes of the American public."

Start with one possible answer to the question, and examine the strengths and weaknesses of this position. Go through any other possible answers to the question, examining their strengths and weaknesses. Then compare and contrast the answers you've evaluated.

> After you have created this outline, the bulk of the work is already finished: You just have to fill in the examples from the text and show how they support your thesis. This technique will steer you away from lengthy digressions, force you to rely upon textual support, and give you a sense of structure that will make the writing go much more quickly.
>
> —Kerry Flannery-Reilly, Princeton
> University

Conclude the paper by summarizing the different positions surrounding the question. How do they answer the question? What still needs to be examined? Or has one of the answers pretty well addressed everything that needs to be said? What does this mean for the human race?

euneirophrenia: bliss enjoyed upon waking from a pleasant dream

DRAFTING YOUR PAPER

Maybe your exemplary research and organization has produced an argument whose brilliance rivals the greatest works of Aristotle and Plato. Its clarity and coherence compete with such gurus of English prose as Strunk and White. Then again, this might not be the case. Maybe only an amorphous idea has surfaced amidst the rough outline you've arranged. If the latter more accurately describes your paper, roll up your sleeves. Try to at least summarize your argument. If you can't, you should return to the outlining and organization chapter.

EXPLAIN YOUR THESIS TO YOUR ROOMMATE

(and Other Tips)

Summarization techniques can help you to clarify your argument. Consider this step the equivalent of creating the Cliffs Notes to your paper. Cliffs Notes, as we're sure you are aware, are organized and coherent. Don't tell us you've never used them. A couple of sentences that describe your main argument and its supporting arguments will suffice. Talking about the theme of your paper can prove to be as beneficial a tactic as these couple of sentences. Feel free to call up your mom and explain it to her. She'll most likely feign an interest (one advantage over your roommate), and the phone call will provide an opportunity to ask her to send you some cookies or cash (another advantage over your roommate). Don't disregard your roomie, however. Explaining your topic and argument to a blank stare won't hurt, either.

Where to Write

Sure, you can draft your paper in the computer lab, the library, or your cluttered desk. Many famous authors, however, have abandoned the traditional writer's stance (room in an attic, author hunched over a loud typewriter) for positions that, for them, provide the conditions best suitable to creative genius.

Robert Frost: sat in a fluffy chair with a writing board set on his lap.

Thomas Wolfe: wrote while standing, using his refrigerator as his desktop.

Hemingway: also wrote while standing, setting his typewriter on his dresser.

Mozart: composed while in bed.

Virginia Woolf: bathed while trying to conceive her next novel.

John Sayles (filmmaker and novelist): gets ideas while swimming.

Irving Stone: overcomes writers' block by gardening and pulling weeds.

Carol Shields: brainstorms while vacuuming.

It might seem anticlimactic, but many students and professors recommend that you leave your paper for a while after researching. Your break can be short (take a shower), long (watch a *Simpsons* episode or two—thank goodness for syndication), longer (watch *Gone with the Wind* in its director's cut), or longer still (go to sleep). Unless you're in "the writing zone" and prepared to crank out your paper, it can be good to give your mind a break.

> I always try to write my papers over the weekend when I have a large block of time. Usually this means spending the week before thinking about my topic as I walk to class, take a shower, or daydream. I find I formulate some of the best ideas when I *don't* have paper in front of me, very frustrating since I can then never remember what I was inspired about!
>
> —Lizzie Adelman, Haverford College,
> comparative literature major

alexipharmic: having the quality or nature of an antidote to poison

So how will this draft take shape? Will you type it on your computer or scribble it on lined paper? Don't automatically assume that typing your draft will speed the drafting process up. In fact, writing your paper by hand may produce a faster and more coherent draft, according to many professors and students.

> I think that the prevalence of poor writing (my own included) is the result of relying wholly on writing directly into the computer. It's then easy to cut and paste, and the process is faster, which often means less time spent absorbing ideas.
>
> —Linda Angst, Professor of Sociology and Anthropology, Earlham College

> I type faster than I write, but I find that my first draft comes out faster if I write it out by hand. Because I type so fast, I don't let myself THINK as deeply about what I'm writing; I put down every thought as it crosses my mind. Consequently, I find that I have to delete and rewrite, delete and rewrite. If I'm writing by hand, I make sure I have a coherent idea before exerting my hand to write out the sentence. Sure, scratch marks still surface in the handwritten paper, but this messy product eliminates all the careless phrases on the computer.
>
> —Anonymous student, University of Michigan

> To get a sense of the big picture and the overall organization of a paper, I find it helpful to scrawl out my paper with a pen. While my roommate cannot understand why I squander my time writing out what I will eventually type, I find that writing out my paper allows me to spread out the papers and see what I've already written. There's only so much you can view on a computer screen. Little additions are easier to insert if you can just write it on a sheet instead of scrolling up and down trying to remember where the relevant section was.
>
> —Anonymous student at University of California, Los Angeles

I always make my undergraduates write their paper by hand. I tell them that I can decipher all handwriting. I do that so the students cannot claim "Typo, Typo." They soon discover that they cannot use Spell Check or Grammar Check. That way I get a much better sense of their writing weaknesses.

—Kenneth Crannell, Professor of
Communication, Emerson College

The biggest problem I have found with my Rice students is that their writing is sloppy and their prose is rambling. In almost all cases, it appears that the students compose their essays directly on their computers and so write in the same haphazard fashion as they speak. I strongly urge them to write the first draft of their essays by hand, and then edit the essays as they type them into their computers. This way, they at least have the opportunity to think a bit as they write, and think again as they edit.

—Colleen Lamos, Associate Professor of
English, Rice University

Not everyone agrees that the handwritten paper is advantageous, however. One student at Pepperdine University found that drafts constructed on the computer are more helpful:

If I'm just plopping down ideas as they come into my head, it's so much better to use my computer. If I just want to get something down on paper but am not satisfied with the clarity of the thought, I can easily distinguish the idea with bold typeface. Later, I can go back, identify all my bold typefaced sentences and revise them individually.

ansible: an interstellar instantaneous communications device

Other students had their own reasons for composing their papers on the computer:

> This might be the lamest excuse for drafting by computer, but I rely heavily on the thesaurus. I often get stumped by finding the proper word, and it's so easy to just push SHIFT-F7 and get the computer to quickly fill in a word for me.
>
> —Anonymous student at Yale University

> I type 80 words per minute. I write about 20 words per minute. Conclusion? I type out my drafts.
>
> —Andrea Chen, Yale University

Whether you're facing a blank computer screen or gazing at the empty lines of your college-ruled paper, you're probably just itching to write or to get some good Chinese take-out . . . and then write. What then?

First, place your thesis in a prominent position. Your thesis *is* your paper, (albeit in an increasingly condensed form). Keep it in sight at all times. Feel free to write your thesis on a card, nail it deeply into your "sticky-tack only" wall, and consistently stare at it. Should you fear the $978.17 fine that your school levies against such offenses, feel free to write the topic on your hand or record it on a Post-it® Note.

DRAFT DODGING

Let's define a *draft*. Pop quiz, hot shot: Which of the following definitions is most relevant to your paper-writing quest?

Draft (n.) 1. a current of air 2. a device in a flue controlling air circulation 3. a pull or traction of a load 4. the selection of personnel from a group, especially conscription for military service 5. a gulp or inhalation 6. a document for transferring money 7. the depth of a vessel's keel below the water line 8. a heavy demand on resources 9. a preliminary outline, plan, or picture; version

Is that your final answer? If your outline contains a bunch of hot air and you chose number 1, that's a bad sign. But we'll assume you chose number 9, unless it's wartime and your number just came up. In that case, this research paper is the least of your worries.

Given that this is just a preliminary plan, you should not concern yourself with style and precision. Fine-tuning isn't necessary in this drafting stage, so don't worry about the grammar, the structure, or any of the amazingly wise proofreading topics offered later. Consideration of these details only confuses and obstructs the writing process. In fact, an obsession with sounding good at this stage is one of the most common causes of writers' block.

Don't get stumped by individual words or an inability to beautifully convey your ideas. If you can't remember the right adjective, put in a space, or put in some sort of marker that indicates that you need to find the appropriate word later.

If you get stuck over individual words, your ideas will never make it into your paper. Just sit down, forget about sounding eloquent, and get your ideas down on paper. Just say what you mean to say.

argopelter: strange mythical creature which lived in hollow trees and spent days throwing things at passersby

Tips for Getting Unblocked

So, a suggestion on how to start: Just start. Often what you write just out of the gate will be edited, changed or even thrown out. Not to worry. Don't get hung up on first sentences, paragraphs, etcetera. Just put something down to get going—write through any block or apprehensions. Once you get going it is much easier to go back and retool anything you don't like.

> —Jordan Smith, freelance writer and
> master's candidate in journalism,
> University of Texas—Austin

For first drafts, turn off the internal censor. Put aside the self-critic for later. Let the writing flow, if possible, for that's how the discoveries happen. Just write. Write until the flow stops (or the flows stop). Then take a break, and come back and see what you've got. Writing blocks usually have to do with this internal censor who pans every word you write. Temporarily shelving that critic—learning to put that voice aside for a time—usually solves the writing block. Other things to try are: specific assignments that take the student in an unexplored direction.

> —Cynthia Hogue, Associate Professor of
> English, Stadler Center for Poetry, Bucknell
> University

Students often straitjacket their writing by premature editing. They have a hard time getting much written on an assignment because they are trying to do two things at once: create, and constructively criticize. Thus it is extremely valuable to firmly distinguish two distinct stages of writing: generating ideas, and editing. Trying to do both simultaneously has the effect of choking off the creative juices. A writer should let himself freely generate ideas for an outline and first draft while postponing self-editing as a completely separate activity. Assure yourself that you *will* later scrutinize your work, quite possibly revising it drastically. But by keeping that critical perspective at bay in the early stages, you will have an easier time generating material.

> —Tara Smith, Associate Professor of
> Philosophy, University of Texas—Austin

> "Then you should say what you mean," the March Hare went on.
>
> "I do," Alice hastily replied; "as least—at least I mean what I say—that's the same thing, you know."
>
> "Not the same thing a bit!" said the Hatter. "Why, you might just as well say that 'I see what I eat' is the same thing as 'I eat what I see'!"
>
> —Lewis Carroll, *Alice in Wonderland*

A note to the procrastinator: Here's where you lose. Time allows you to write this first draft unencumbered by grammatical and stylistic concerns. Without time to invest in multiple drafts, however, you'll have to worry about those details *while* you write your rough draft.

> Writer's block is a fancy term made up by whiners so they can have an excuse to drink alcohol.
>
> —Steve Martin

Talking through your ideas can aid the process of recording your ideas on paper. Terrence Doody, Professor of English at Rice University recommends talking during the drafting stage: "I ask [my students] what they meant to say and they can explain it quite well out loud in their natural speaking voice. I also require the students to have a writing partner, who is their audience and who will read the paper back out loud so they can hear their prose. This works to eliminate passive voice, dangling participles, alien vocabulary, untoward rhythms."

Similarly, don't worry about the intro and conclusion at this point in the writing process. Your attention should center on designing coherent and simple paragraphs that advance your argument. Crafting a creative opening might not be appropriate at this point, especially if you're not quite sure what direction the paper will take. Some students, however, like to write their introductions at this stage since they use their introduction as a check to make sure they know exactly what they're about to say.

autohagiography: writing about oneself in an adulatory way

First-Draft Tips from Students

Worrying about individual words or elegant phrasing when you're drafting is unproductive. Just write what you want to write, and do it quickly, so that you can have some semblance of a paper to work with. If you're worrying about whether *disgust* or *aversion* sounds better at this stage, you'll never get anywhere. First, you'll most likely be so consumed with these superficial details that you'll ignore the more critical issues like "Am I making a valid point supported with details?" and "Does this answer the question?" Second, you'll spend hours and hours with only a couple paragraphs to show for it.

—Anonymous student at Grinnell College

If you can't think of anything to write, play Tetris. It works the other side of your brain, giving the writing side some time to cool off.

—Caroline Marvin, Yale University, English major

Rituals, caffeine, sleeping, and watching an episode or two won't work. The best way to gain inspiration during the draft process is to inspire yourself. Just start writing. The phrases and fragments you come up with will surprise you and lead to new ideas.

—Jonathan Soverow, Princeton University

People often get stuck into trying to write a perfect paper, and agonize over things such as word choice and style.

—Ashley Brown, Dartmouth University

[When I'm short on time] I tend to just get on the computer and write everything that I can think of. After all my ideas are down, it's so easy to rearrange and modify them. I make sure to evaluate everything I've written and make sure I'm not leaving in anything unnecessary. It's easy either to overlook a sentence or two that doesn't apply to the material or to restate something.

This is the best way for me to write last-minute essays, because usually the factor that keeps me from doing them is just the fear of not getting them done. Once I have written the number of pages I need, I feel better. Then I can relax and do a better job.

—Stephanie Obodda, Princeton University

> Before I delve into my paper, I like to know exactly what I'm about to say. Condensing my argument into an introduction is a useful exercise before I begin my body paragraphs. Most of the time, I significantly alter this introduction after the paper's written, however.
>
> —Anonymous student at Washington University

> If, during the process of outlining the paper, I've come up with a catchy opening statement, I'll include an introduction in the rough draft. Most of the time, however, I find that stressing over a well-constructed opening before I've written the body of the paper is . . . well, stressful.
>
> —Anonymous student at Colorado State University

Ignoring the finer points of the essay like style, grammar, and introductions, however, is not license to completely check out. This draft should follow some structure, and you should constantly evaluate how well you're supporting or developing your paper's thesis. Following some structure and staying thesis-centered is easy if you pay special attention to topic sentences, paragraphs, and your outline (assuming you have one).

TOPIC SENTENCES AND PARAGRAPHING
(or Your Paper's Just Fine with Strong Opening Lines)

A paragraph is a group of facts, arguments, evidences, or descriptions that develop a single idea. Your outline should express what these individual ideas are and what the content of each paragraph should be. It's difficult to prescribe a certain length to a paragraph. Paragraph length will depend on the depth of your argument, the amount of evidence you need to provide, or the number of facts that support the paragraph's single idea. One rule of thumb, however, is to make sure your paragraph length is proportional to both the length of the paper and the

borborygmus: rumbling in the guts

length of the other paragraphs. If your paper is three pages long, your full-page paragraph may need to be subdivided. If, on the other hand, your paper is twenty-seven pages long, a paragraph that spans a page may be acceptable. If the single page paragraph is surrounded by two paragraphs of two sentences, you should aim at balancing them.

The ideal paragraph structure should resemble a quality double-decker hamburger: a thick bun, thick patty, thick bun, thick patty, thick bun, etcetera. If your paragraphs more closely resemble a 39-cent McDonalds hamburger with superthin patties, you should consider whether the thinner paragraphs are really parts of a larger paragraph. On the other hand, longer paragraphs may need to be subdivided.

I like students to try to get three "details" or pieces of evidence in each paragraph.

—Thomas Gustafson, Associate Professor of English, University of Southern California

The quickest way I can tell a student has struggled with a piece of writing is to look at the paragraphs. Students working frantically against a deadline, or who aren't intellectually in control of their material, will try to smash more and more information into their paragraphs—until the paragraphs become massive blocks of information that are difficult for the reader to digest.

People cut up their meat before they eat it because their digestive system can more readily handle bite-sized food. Same thing with information and paragraphing. Learning to see the paragraph as a single unit of thought can help simplify writing.

Therefore, I tell students to remember Ziomek's 1-2-3-4-5 Rule on Paragraphing: one thought, expressed in no more than two or three sentences, and consuming up to four or five lines on a word processor screen.

—Jon Ziomek, Assistant Dean for Graduate Editorial Programs, Northwestern University

The most important element of every paragraph is its topic sentence. Close attention to topic sentences will direct your reader, ensure organization, prevent common paragraph errors, guard against repeated information, and protect against pure summary.

> Your argument must proceed in a logical progression from one thought to the next. This logic should be clear within your sentences, from one sentence to the next, and from one paragraph to the next. Every paragraph must have a topic sentence that presents the paragraph's main idea. The main idea cannot be merely the topic of that paragraph; rather, it must communicate the point that you need to make within the logical progression of your paper. In other words, the topic sentence should be a "mini-thesis." Everything your thesis does with respect to your paper, your topic sentence should do with respect to your paragraph. In order to clarify your logical progression from one paragraph to the next, every topic sentence should contain a transition that connects the idea of the preceding paragraph to the idea of the present paragraph.
>
> —Jeannine DeLombard, Professor of
> English, University of Puget Sound

As you write, therefore, carefully consider each topic sentence. The topic sentence can be considered your paragraph's thesis: It should encapsulate the content of its paragraph. The reader should be able to identify the contents of the paragraph based on reading this sentence. Charles T. Wood, professor at Dartmouth University, explains the function of a topic sentence: "The paragraph's first or topic sentence serves the same function for the paragraph as does the first paragraph for the paper as a whole."

The importance of a succinct and descriptive topic sentence is evidenced in the grading criteria that the Green River Community College gives its professors:

omphaloskepsis: contemplating one's navel as an aid to meditation

A paper earns an A if:

1. The title, central idea of the whole paper, and topic sentences of the various paragraphs combine to give an adequate summary of the paper.
2. The central idea is evident and is adhered to throughout the paper.
3. Each topic sentence supports the thesis sentence.

Leora Auslander, Associate Professor of History at the University of Chicago, explains one of the key expectations she has of her students: "Learn what a topic paragraph and sentence are and use them!"

When outlining, some people find it helpful to write out a complete topic sentence for each projected paragraph and then list the examples and ideas that will be contained within the paragraph.

Not only will carefully constructed topic sentences make your paper more organized, but they will help you evaluate how well your paragraphs connect to your thesis. When crafting your topic sentence, remember some of the common functions of a good topic sentence:

- To present new evidence or insightful ideas that strengthen and substantiate your thesis
- To give the audience the necessary background information that will help them understand your argument
- To defend and address counterarguments that might be presented by critic
- To explain ideas in your arguments

Probably every college student will see a "too much summary" comment in the margin of his paper at one point in his academic career. Whether you're arguing or merely summarizing can usually be discovered by reading the topic sentence of a paragraph.

To make sure that your essay has not fallen into a series of summaries that never quite move toward analysis, check your topic sentences, which are often but not always the lead sentence or two in a paragraph. If you're using a lot of *time* words (such as "next," "after," "then") or *listing* words (such as "also," "another," "in addition"), you are very likely only describing the source text rather than building an argument by analyzing the text. Keep in mind that if you follow the chronology of a source text, you always need to show that there's a reason for doing so, and that the reason comes from the logic of your argument, not of that of the source text.

—Elizabeth Abrams, Writing Fellow at
Harvard University

Scrutinizing topic sentences is a helpful tool for making sure you're not repeating information unnecessarily. Check to make sure each of your topic sentences is distinct from others. If you notice that some topic sentences are suspiciously similar to other paragraphs' topic sentences, chances are that those paragraphs might have dangerously similar contents. For example, if one paragraph's topic sentence says something like "While they may be delectable delights, chicken fingers are bad for your health" and the following paragraph's topic sentence says something like "Because they are fried chunks of artificial meat product, chicken fingers are not good for your heart," you probably are repeating information.

If that's the case, you need to 1) eliminate some of your sentences, or 2) merge the two paragraphs. While a search for repeated information is a crucial step in editing, being aware of repetition in the drafting stage can save you some work later. It will also save you from professors' criticism.

Undergraduates seem to believe that anything worth saying once is worth saying twice.

—Ken Bode, Dean of the Medill School of
Journalism at Northwestern University

callithumpian: relating to a band of discordant instruments or a noisy parade

Top-Ten Ways to Overcome Writer's Block

As suggested by student responses.

1. Go out for a walk and enjoy the fresh air, leaving your paper behind. If you go to school in New Haven, lie down and dream about what it would be like to breathe fresh air and be able to walk outside alone.

2. Stoke up on strong coffee.

3. Give it a rest and come back to it later.

4. Drop that silly English class and become a science major.

5. Lower your standards and keep going (or start). It's better to sit in front of the computer and type "I have nothing to write" over and over than it is to get up and find something else to do. You'll get bored pretty quickly and discover that you do have something to say. But in serious cases, psychotherapy may help.

6. Go out, sit on any given town corner and talk to bums. We have a bum who sprinkles glitter on the sidewalk in front of our dance club. He wears a Viking helmet and gives the "shhhh" finger-to-lips gesture when you catch him doing it. Write about that. Write about bums. It clears a blocked brain right up.

7. Talk about the subject with anyone who will listen.

8. Usually I bang my head on the keyboard, scream, then punch the monitor. It worked the two times I wrote anything.

9. Sleep on it.

10. Accept that you're going to flunk out of school and become a full-time ski/beach bum.

Because your topic sentence identifies the contents of its paragraph, most of the time the topic sentence will be placed in the first or second sentences of the paragraph. While this location is the most popular place to orient your topic sentence, some academic writing allows you to build up to an argument and place your topic sentence as the last sentence of the paragraph.

HOW TO USE QUOTES

Quotes are an important part of any well-researched academic paper. Here's how to use them correctly.

1. When you include a quote that is an independent clause or an entire sentence:
   a. Precede quotes with commas.

   Example
   Wombats have overinflated egos; one wombat from Iowa was overheard exclaiming, "Humans underestimate my unrivaled, fantastic intelligence."

   b. Capitalize the first letter of the quote.

   Example
   Hockey players also have large egos; the goalie from Yale declared, "My hair looks fantastic!"

2. Keep end punctuation inside the quote. You learned this in elementary school, silly.

   Incorrect
   Johnny said, "Hot diggity! Let's go to the store"!

   Correct
   Johnny said, "Hot diggity! Let's go to the store!"

3. When your quote is not an entire sentence, don't worry about the commas or capitalization.

   Example
   She said that she was "incredibly afraid of gibbering monkeys."

deipnosophist: a master of dinner-table conversation

4. Aim to keep the quote in its most original form. When incorporating quotes, it can be tempting to change the wording slightly. To make things fit into your past tense paper, it can be easy to change that *is* to *was*. Sometimes you might want to replace an *I* with *she*.

   a. Try to change your text around to accommodate the exact quote.

   Example
   She said that "I am a genius."
   OR: She claimed, "I am a genius."

   b. When a change in your text is impossible, you can resort to brackets.

   Example
   She said that "[she was] a genius."

5. You may need to include brackets to replace nondescript pronouns.

   Example
   He exclaimed, "It was the ugliest thing I'd seen in my life."
   He exclaimed, "[My reflection in the mirror] was the ugliest thing I'd seen in my life."

6. Keep quotes condense. Cite only the most powerful phrases and the most relevant information. Sometimes you'll find a couple quotable sentences. There might be some irrelevant information tucked into one of the sentences. Feel free to replace unnecessary phrases with ellipses (...).

7. Be selective with your quotes. Don't quote something that is not remarkable. To say that Historian Higgins said, "World War II was a tragic event," is not an effective use of a quote. Quotes that have an especially descriptive portrayal, insightful idea, or nicely constructed wording, however, make poignant quotes. Use your better judgement in identifying how beneficial a quote is.

8. Use quotes if an idea is unbelievable. While "it was an ugly day in the neighborhood," doesn't qualify for being a beautiful, insightful, or descriptive quote, you might want to use it if you're claiming that Mr. Rogers said it. Most readers will refuse to accept a statement like "Mr. Rogers thought that it was an ugly day in the neighborhood." Your reader will be less skeptical, however, if you say "Mr. Rogers told producers that 'it's an ugly day in the neighborhood, you jerks!'"

9. Don't abuse quotes. Remember that you're the one writing this paper and that you must contribute your own words. Short quotes, ones that are "especially insightful," can be effective.

10. Avoid block quotes. Block quotes are long quotes that need to be separated from the paragraph. Only when the quote is absolutely imperative to describing a situation or when especially effective in proving your point should you include these block quotes. If you can explain or summarize some of the quote, do so. If you are convinced that citing an entire quote will portray, say, exactly what that prisoner was feeling or that will give thorough statistical evidence of the prisoner's history, be sure the quote is inserted according to the following guidelines:

   • Block quotes are those that take up more than three lines on your paper or that are more than one paragraph in length. These quotes need to be separated from the text.
   • Go to a new line.
   • Indent the quote by an additional five spaces on the left margin.
   • Sometimes the indented quote is put in a smaller font (i.e., if your paper is in 12-point font, the block quote may be 10 points).
   • Do not surround the quote with quotation marks. Separating it and indenting it will indicate that it's a quote.

So let's say you're writing your 35-page manifesto on how pistachio ice cream should be banned from stores across the country. If you were to put in a block quote from the President of the Chocolate Chip Cookie Dough Ice Cream Coalition (CCCDICC), it might look a little bit like this:

gallimaufry: a hotchpotch, jumble, or confused medley

Pistachio ice cream cannot fill the ice cream parlors, the kitchen's freezer, or the grocery stores of the United States of America. Its color is despicable, and its taste is even worse. I'd prefer to eat frozen cardboard. We cannot let our children waste away by eating this despised flavor. SAVE OUR CHILDREN! Purge the pistachio! (Higgins 163)

Then you'd return to writing about why pistachio ice cream is the food of felons by returning to your paper's normal format.

11. Delay citing your quotes. You should make a note of where you've found these quotes (hopefully you've documented that kind of stuff while researching), but don't trouble yourself with adding in footnotes or endnotes while drafting. If your professor wants simple parenthetical quotes, however, these should be inserted as you're writing your paper.

BEYOND THE BODY

Once you've finished drafting the body of your paper, incorporating quotes to brilliant effect, go back and write a conclusion and introduction. While the intro and conclusion can be a tremendous challenge, your paper cannot spontaneously begin defending or reputing an idea; it needs an introduction that will prepare and a conclusion that will summarize and remind your reader of the paper's purpose.

A useful organizational device for short and midlength student papers is the old saw, "tell 'em what you're going to tell 'em, tell 'em, then tell 'em what you told 'em." In other words, begin the paper with an introductory paragraph providing the reader with a road map, and conclude the paper with a paragraph summarizing the argument. Develop the overall argument of the paper in the body (i.e., tell 'em).

—William Connelly, John K. Boardman
Politics Professor, Washington and Lee
University

INTRODUCTIONS

The introduction is a crucial component of the paper because it provides an outline of the paper. A good introduction will explain the subject of the paper, suggest why it is important, and provide a road map of your approach to the topic. Elements of a good road map will include the background that equips your reader for an understanding of the topic, the argument that you will espouse throughout the paper, and a brief explanation of how you will defend this argument. After reading the introduction, your reader should be able to anticipate the direction of the rest of your paper.

You'd like your reader to anticipate an exciting and organized paper. Since you never get a second chance to make a good first impression, a carefully constructed introduction is important to a paper of any length. The reader who sees a vague, disorganized, dull introduction will expect the same quality in the body of the paper. If your introduction is direct, concise, and engaging, however, the reader will expect the same of the subsequent paragraphs.

> Whereas students often begin essays by stating a thesis or idea, a better idea is to start by summarizing what someone else has said about the topic or, even better, by describing a controversy over it. Such an opening "sets up" your own intervention in the discussion and makes it clear why you find it necessary to write the paper in the first place. In real-world communication, after all, we assume writers have some urgent point that makes them write, and sketching in the prior conversation on your subject is the usual way to indicate that point. When a paper makes no reference to any conversation that it's seeking to enter, it tends to degenerate into a series of statements in a vacuum, and is vulnerable to questions like "So what?" and "Who cares?"
>
> —Gerald Graff, Dean of Curriculum and Pedagogy, University of Illinois

footle: to waste time; act foolish

State the argument clearly (whether it's a question you are asked to answer or a general problem of the text). Then, in the first paragraph, be very explicit about how you will proceed in the paper to answer the question. If you disagree with the proposition or the argument in the text, tell why and offer your resolution.

—Linda Angst, Professor of Sociology and Anthropology, Earlham College

Effective introductions will begin with attention-grabbers.

I still tell students what my mother drummed into me when I first began writing something in elementary school: Begin an essay with an interesting first sentence that captures the reader's attention.

—Thomas Gustafson, Associate Professor of English, University of Southern California

Inviting openers:

1. An intriguing example

2. A provocative quotation

3. A surprising scenario

4. A related anecdote

5. An insightful question

Don't try to amuse your reader in the first sentence. Attention-grabbers can be engaging without being cutesy and dumb. Impress your reader by convincing him or her that your paper is worthy of attention.

Your introduction should begin with a general or abstract idea. Gradually "funnel" your opening; each succeeding sentence should narrow the subject. The final sentence will, in most cases, be your thesis. Your thesis will be the least general statement; it should be concise, direct, and specific.

What Not to Do in the Introduction

1. Avoid truisms. Don't bore your reader with self-evident "truths." Anything that goes without saying shouldn't be said. Sweepingly general statements like "there can be no doubt," "down through history," "it's clear that," should serve as red flags for pointless paragraph padding. Tell your reader something less colloquial and more insightful.

> Among the most annoying pet peeves are students who begin their essays with a statement that purports to explain the world. It goes something like this, "Ever since the beginning of time, philosophers (statesmen, etcetera)...." Not only is this almost [always] false, but even if true, almost no one can support such a statement.
>
> —Barry Shain, Associate Professor of
> Political Science, Colgate University

2. Don't complain about the challenge of writing on the assigned topic. "Who am I to consider so profound a problem that has plagued historians for centuries.... "

3. Eliminate Webster-mania. An obvious dictionary definition will bore your reader. "Before considering the sonnets of Shakespeare, one must consider what love is. Webster's New Collegiate Dictionary offers this definition...."

4. Don't offer facts that no one needs to be reminded of. "George Washington, the first president of the United States of America...."

5. Avoid platitudes. While they might be true, they're boring and unnecessary.
   "The processes of life are awe inspiring."

6. Don't reveal an insecurity or lack of knowledge about a topic. "Locke's theories are a challenge to comprehend entirely, but I will attempt to...."

7. Don't blatantly announce your plan of attack. Be subtle. "In this paper, I will...."

> **furbelow:** a gathered strip or pleated border; showy ornaments or trimmings

CONCLUSIONS

Your conclusion is your last chance to have the last word. Making a good final impression is as vital as making a good first impression. To invest time and effort into your intro, thesis, argument, style, structure, and evidence without investing equal energy in a conclusion would not be wise. Don't let your conclusion fizzle out; capitalize on this last opportunity to convince your reader that you've effectively proven your thesis. Your conclusion will collect and summarize your ideas, demonstrate their importance, and propel your reader to further examination. Remember that your professor will be grading your paper immediately after he or she reads your last sentence; go out with gusto.

> I look for conclusions that say something more than the opening paragraph, and I encourage students to leave me with a new thought at the end of a paper.
>
> —Thomas Gustafson, Associate Professor of English, University of Southern California

The conclusion offers you the chance to expand on the topic. You may consider related issues, establish new connections, and elaborate on your findings. Your conclusion should answer the reader's "so what?" Whatever information will answer this question may be included in the conclusion.

> The conclusion is generally a good place for summing up, showing how the points you've raised support, negate, or offer a compromise to the original problem.
>
> —Linda Angst, Professor of Sociology and Anthropology, Earlham College

Chapter Four

Ways to end your paper:

1. Make a useful analogy or comparison.

2. Suggest specific actions that the reader should take in light of your discovery.

3. Speculate on the future implications of your thesis.

What Your Conclusion Should Not Do:

1. Don't end with a hollow cliché.
   "King Lear shows us that there's no fool like an old fool."

2. Don't make unnecessary announcements.
   "In conclusion, let me remind you...."

3. Don't allow the paper to fizzle out.
   "Research has prompted much discovery that will enable future development."

4. Don't make a lofty claim.
   "This discovery of wombats' natural affinity for frozen novelties will forever change the direction of scientific research."

5. Don't repeat your thesis and main points.

---

inglenook: a chimney corner

In your conclusion, discuss the patterns you found in the evidence, and what you learned about the central subject matter that concerned you to begin with. In your conclusions, you will be speaking generally, once again, but you will be focusing on issues as they appeared and developed in the evidence as a whole. Once again, careful readers will have been getting hints, but there is no reason for you to be repetitive in your conclusion since you are doing something entirely new.

—J. David Parker, Professor of History,
Washington and Lee University

Students often feel compelled in the conclusions of their essays to write about contemporary issues and these remarks almost invariably are not entailed by the evidence adduced and instead are an opportunity for a student to express personal opinions. They should instead be saved for the student newspaper or conversations with their parents and friends.

—Barry Shain, Associate Professor of
Political Science, Colgate University

On that note, we'll conclude this chapter.

THE REVISION PROCESS

Re•vise (n.) 1.To prepare a newly edited version of (a text); 2.To reconsider and change or modify: I have revised my opinion of him.

So you've written your paper. Congratulations. We've got some bad news, however: Your paper-writing process is not quite finished. Sure, you've finished a lap around the track in good time, but if you want to win the mile, you have three more ahead of you. But alas, stressing out about your 800-meter splits can't be your sole preoccupation right now. Instead, you should be focusing on revision.

WHY REVISE?

"But after cranking out a 12-page draft, I'm too exhausted to edit. It's done, and that's all that matters," you might whine. Or perhaps you're thinking, "Why revise? This thing doesn't look too bad to me, and the spell check doesn't seem to have a problem with it." It's likely that you'd be content if you never had to read another word on the U.S. government's motivation for dropping an atom bomb, or the smirk of Mona Lisa, or Greek theater. Perhaps after skimming through your draft, you fear that a more thorough revision would uncover some serious flaws that you have neither the time nor energy to handle. Hard-core editing might be your greatest nightmare.

A former student recently e-mailed me the following: "Professor Booth, I had a dream about you last night. Having died, you appeared before St. Peter, at the Gate. He looked at you in a friendly way, but then said, "I'm sorry, Professor Booth, but we'll need at least one more draft."

—Wayne Booth, George M. Pullman
Distinguished Service, Professor
Emeritus in English Language and
Literature, University of Chicago

It's at this desperate point that you should recall Patrick Henry and his dramatic "give me liberty or give me death" speech. Did Patrick Henry and his compatriots ever give up? By God they did not. We "know not what course others may take," but as for you, you will finish off the solid work you've begun by polishing the paper and making it coherent and articulate.

Work-work-work
Till the brain begins to swim;
Work-work-work
Till the eyes are heavy and dim.

—Thomas Hood,
"The Song of the Shirt"

It took Neil Simon an entire year just to publish a first draft of *Come Blow Your Horn*. His revising efforts lasted two and a half years. He explained that "there was barely any similarity between the first draft and the twenty-second. The play was so primitive in its earliest versions, it bordered on Neanderthal." Simon would put his draft into a desk drawer for weeks on end before returning to revise it.

At that point, the words no longer seem to come from me but rather it's as though some unknown person had sent it to me through the mail, asking my opinion of it. As I read it, what's good remains good, but what's bad jumps off the page and smacks me right across my ego. My thick black indelible pen puts a line through every inferior word and sentence, blocking it out forever for any theater historian who might find it one day and say, "How could he write such crap?"

—Neil Simon

sockdolager: a heavy or knock-down blow

Your eraser will be as important an instrument as your pencil, and your backspace key might be the most commonly pressed on your keyboard. The value of revising cannot be overstated, although you may think differently by the end of this chapter.

> Whatever sentence will bear to be read twice, we may be sure was thought twice.
>
> —Henry David Thoreau

Thorough revision produces a polished and precise draft that your professor will appreciate (translation: You will get a good grade). But don't take our word for it; listen to the professors who repeatedly emphasize the benefits of editing and proofreading.

I try to impress upon my students that developing the skill to write well is a lifetime effort. My favorite technique in demonstrating that point is to show the students a heavily blue-penciled draft, using an overhead, and then go over the editor's improvements in style. Then I point out that the pages that we have been discussing are from one of my published works. The exercise, which comes after I return corrected papers of theirs, puts their efforts in perspective.

—Russell J. Leng, Jermain Professor of
Political Economy and International Law,
Middlebury College

The most important extra thing is drafts. If professors can build a draft due-date into the syllabus for all important papers, with at least a week between that date and the final due-date, much good will arise.

—Kidder Smith, Professor of History and
Asian Studies, Bowdoin University

My advisor kept telling me, "Good writing is rewriting."

—A. J. Guarino, Professor of Education,
Auburn University

Rewrite, rewrite. That's what the pros do. Amateurs tend not to.

—George Harmon, Professor of
Journalism, Northwestern University

Spew-Revise-Spew-Revise, and Other Tips from Students

Many times students will simply write a paper, failing to concentrate on their arguments. This problem can be easily solved in the revision process; if the student realizes that the reader should be persuaded by the points presented in the paper, then the student can focus on supporting their specific arguments (rather than revising to add length to the paper). For example, adding quotes to support a point of view can be very effective (although it might require additional research). The student should revise from the point of view of a reader, concentrating on strengthening arguments.

—Robert Edward Lee IV, Davidson College, Spanish major

No, normal college students don't edit their papers if they finish at three in the morning. We are lacking sleep already. However, it would probably make sense to edit these papers more, seeing that we have probably already written half of the paper in a caffeine-induced frenzy.

—Denise Minor, University of North Carolina—Chapel Hill, business administration major

I usually write between 10–15 drafts per paper. (I'm a perfectionist, so if I didn't force myself to spew crap I'd never write anything. Therefore I spew-revise-spew-revise-revise-revise...ad infinitum...ad nauseum) That's it—same approach every time, regardless of how much I've procrastinated (which I've learned that I can't do—if I run out of time and have to hand in a paper that has only been through eight drafts, then it's really bad).

—Amanda Doster, Brown University, English major

steganography: the art of creating and transmitting hidden messages

Students who want to learn how to write must do it often, both in and out of the classroom. Students who want to learn how to write must approach the skill just as an athlete approaches a new physical challenge. Great skaters, dancers, and baseball players often didn't start out great. They practiced day after day until the skill became quite natural.

—Michael Lane, Assistant Professor of Journalism and Public Information, Emerson College

Plan enough time to review and revise the first draft. Generally the payoff is big.

—Linda Angst, Professor of Sociology and Anthropology, Earlham College

Don't be afraid to rewrite and rewrite. Shuffle words and paragraphs around until the paper says what you want it to say. . . . Writing is a craft, and good craftsmanship is valued.

—John Bendix, Professor of Women's Studies, University of Pennsylvania

Since professors cite revision as one of the most valuable elements to writing, it is not surprising that students' refusal to seriously edit their papers ranks among professors' top pet peeves:

Like Don Quixote, I try year after year to teach undergraduates to write rigorous, compelling arguments in crystal clear English. Sometimes I actually take out a windmill or two: Sometimes I get a paper that delivers. The biggest obstacle standing in my way is that students are unwilling to carry out the sustained, painstaking rewriting that is the key to writing a cogent argument. My suspicion, after 15 years of laboring without even a Sancho Panza to help, is that computers and the Internet are working against me. The world of information trains students to rapidly process shallow tidbits over and over. I want my students working with a pencil, pondering the same paragraph for 30 minutes.

—Selmer Bringsjord, Professor of Philosophy, Psychology, and Cognitive Science at Rensselaer Polytechnic Institute

My biggest frustration with students is their unwillingness to take seriously what they write. I suggest to them that they read their sentences aloud before submission to me so that they can tell how the language sounds, what it means, and if they want to say that.

—Graham Russell Hodges, Professor of History, Colgate University

It disturbs me when I have spent a considerable amount of time working to unravel and correct a student's paper and suspect that I have put more time into it than the student.

—Lynn Marie Hoffman, Professor of Education, Bucknell University

The only way to learn to write is to revise, a procedure students do not understand in part because they delay writing most critical (argumentative) essays until the night before. So the trick is to build in artificial deadlines to facilitate revision and rereading (preferably with several days in between each rereading so that the essay is read "cold"). In short, if the task is broken down—topic first, then a thesis, then a brief thesis statement or abstract (100 words), then a rough draft, and revision of the rough draft, all submitted to the instructor—the student (or the writer) has a reasonable chance of writing successfully and effectively.

—Jane Chance, Professor of English, Rice University

So it's hard to contest: Repeated revision reaps renowned, rewardable, right writing. See—had we revised, we would have made sure no sentences like that last truly atrocious one actually made it into our final draft. Good editing will eliminate the extraneous ideas and awkward phrasing that make the first sentence especially annoying. Before you launch into a massive revision effort, bear in mind that now is not the time to become defensive about your writing. Don't throw away a gem of an idea that just needs a little polishing. This paragraph's horribly alliterative introduction, for example, could be heralded as an amazing tongue-twister, and we could beg our editors to keep it in since we spent so long deriving it. Okay, we admit it. Our introductory sentence is foolishly convoluted and complex. We're just including it to prove a point: When you're revising, nothing is sacred. Be willing to change, even to change drastically.

stillicide: the steady drip of a raindrop

Change Is Good

REAL writing is knowing who the reader is and working really hard—using precise wording, conversational phrasing, interesting anecdotes—to get your idea across. That means rewriting, unfortunately: unfortunate in that most writers HATE to change anything in their writing because they look at it as their offspring, as if it can do no wrong (like I feel about my children).

> —George Sylvie, Associate Professor of
> Journalism, University of Texas—Austin

I find there's a rule of thumb: Your "best" line (or your favorite part) usually has to be cut. It's often the place where the language got away from you—came too easily, and therefore you're attached to it. (It has the feel of a revelation without the impact, often enough.)

> —Cynthia Hogue, Director, Stadler Center for
> Poetry, Associate Professor of English
> Bucknell University

To react really poorly to criticism of writing and suggestions on how to improve writing is a sure formula for never improving. Writing well is a process of constant improvement. It is imperative that students understand this and learn to work with, instead of react against, criticisms of their writing. It helps to remember that even well-respected and well-established writers work with editors to improve their writing. It is part of becoming a true writer.

> —Jordan Smith, freelance writer and master's candidate in journalism, University of
> Texas—Austin

Students hate to remove wonderful paragraphs that are well written, but fail to advance the argument of the essay. They must learn to buck up and recognize that all writers have hundreds of pages of wonderful paragraphs that had to be sacrificed for the benefit of the essay.

> —Barry Shain, Professor of Political Science,
> Colgate University

Making changes and eliminating your pet sentences will be easier if you take a break before beginning the revising process.

> The best proofreading tip is to let a paper set for a time after you have "finished." Later (the later the better) pick it up again and read aloud. Leaving a paper distances the writer from the written and makes the writer more objective. I have taken up papers, kept them for three days, and returned them unmarked to students. Then I instruct the students to use the paper as a draft and write a new revised version. All of the revisions are remarkably better than the originals.
>
> —Charlotte Weiss Perlin, Writing Center
> Director, University of Miami

FIVE STRATEGIES FOR REVISING

So you're about to break the wine bottle of revision on the side of the great ship that is your paper and embark on a voyage of editing. As you pull up anchor, remember that, according to writing specialists at Hunter College, "Revising is not a punishment invented by English teachers; it is a process which demands that you see your writing as a reader will see it so that you can shape your writing for a reader."

Many people have their own brilliant strategies for revising papers. Choose whatever method allows you to be most probing and critical. You want to see your paper slathered with as many scratch marks, arrows, caret marks, and little suggestions as you, your roommate, your professor, your writing tutor, your pet hamster, or any other rough-draft reader can muster. Remember that every criticism presented at this stage is one less criticism received on the final draft. So without further ado, we present (in Dolby Surround Sound), five great revising tips.

Strategy 1: Get Others' Help

You always knew being popular would pay off: The more people you can convince to read your paper, the better. Each individual has his or her own strengths, weaknesses, and different colored pens. Find a grammar guru who's especially

strabismus: cross-eyedness

knowledgeable about comma splices or a contentious debater who's prone to proffer countless counterarguments. Receiving a variety of critiques will allow you to strengthen your paper.

In addition to getting a diverse array of comments and suggestions, having others read your paper allows you to get a more objective opinion. Thanks to the fact that you've invested some serious time and brainpower into crafting this near-master-piece, you're practically a blood relative of this paper. Little grammar mistakes might escape your tiring eyes, and missed arguments may not be entirely obvious. A reader who is more distanced from the writing will be more likely to spot these oversights. Readers can also alert you to areas that are unclear or confusing.

Another good reason to get someone else to read your paper: Maybe your reader's smart and you're just a couple fries short of a happy meal. Just kidding.

So whom should you ask to read your paper?

Your Professor or Teaching Assistant

Getting your grader to read your paper in advance is the ideal situation. First, he or she is familiar with the topic and will be able to provide further references, explain factual errors or misunderstandings, redirect wandering ideas—you know, all that good, juicy information. Second, you'll have the opportunity to *talk* about the paper with your professor, which is always a helpful learning tool. Third, you'll have the opportunity to show your prof that, despite the fact that you didn't read last week's required 400 pages, you're relatively responsible. Fourth, if there's one person whose opinion you want, it's your prof. Getting your professor's comments ahead of time will help you better understand his or her expectations. Plus, getting help from your professor forces you to write the paper earlier.

> Being a chronic procrastinator, it often helps if I make goals and stick with them. For instance, Brown has a writing center where undergrads, grad students, faculty, and staff can have a paper, essay, chapter of a thesis, application, article, speech, etcetera read and discussed one-on-one with a Writing Center Associate (grad student or professor). Making an appointment at the center a couple of weeks before the paper is due is a great motivation to complete the essay. By finishing the essay at least a week in

advance, you have plenty of time for thorough revision and editing. You could also schedule an appointment with your professor or TA: Usually they are more than happy to go over any questions or basic concerns regarding research papers.

—Casey China, Brown University

Students often take advice of professors and TAs on how to improve their writing extremely literally, often incorporating verbatim the suggestions of professors as written. This is inappropriate and unacceptable. The idea is to get the student to actually think about these suggestions, use his or her own voice and mind, and work with, or even reject suggestions, based on his or her own assessments. It is very frustrating when suggestions are incorporated as if they were original student thought.

—Jordan Smith, freelance writer and master's candidate in journalism, University of Texas—Austin

Writing Tutors

Most universities have writing centers that offer student or faculty assistance. Tutors are an invaluable resource, since they've read numerous papers and know what is expected of solid academic writing. If you can choose among the writing tutors, check into their background. A political philosophy professor will probably be best prepared to advise you on your paper on Machiavelli's infatuation with Rice-a-Roni, the San Francisco Treat, while a senior engrossed in his thesis on Elizabethan comedy will be able to provide insight into your paper on Shakespearean insults.

Your Parents

Don't scoff at this suggestion. Some parents are eager to help out—they like to know that you're learning stuff and that their big bucks are going toward something besides midnight pizza runs. Plus, your mother is a smart woman.

surrebutter: a formal response by a plaintiff in a court case

Talk to someone (I call my Mom) about the topics you're writing on. Tell them what you know, why it's important, why it's interesting, etcetera. Get comfortable with the topic.

—Emily Jamie, Smith College, psychology major

My mom is an awesome editor. If I have a really important paper, I will get her feedback on it. She really knows what she is doing.

—Elizabeth Herman, Cornell University

Your Friends

Your pals can be great prospects for reading your papers, if you can get them to stop playing NHL 2000 on the Playstation.

Not that your friends are inconsiderate and unwilling to help you out, but let's be realistic. They've got work to do and might not be terribly interested in your essay recounting recent examples of sociopathic political cynicism. So, work out one of those "you scratch my back, I'll scratch yours" arrangements. Hey, you stand a chance of learning something new about your friend's paper topic. And learning, my friend, is what this whole college business is all about.

Make the necessary revisions, print out another hard copy, and find a friendly (preferably good-looking) English major to make grammatical corrections.

—Brad Olson, Harvard University, government major

Who do I go to for editing? Mainly peers, roommates, etcetera. But you have to be careful who you pick. For instance, I know of a couple people who will just read your paper and tell you that they think it's good. And then I know a couple of other people who get really into editing papers and making suggestions. My suggestion: Find a good friend who will really *read* the paper and give good comments.

—Denise Minor, University of North Carolina, Chapel Hill, business administration major

Your Classmates

Not that your classmates must be distinguished from your friends, but really; none of your friends are taking that class on the culture of Kazakhstanian shepherds. The best critic of your paper will be people who are familiar with the topic.

> I had always placed great emphasis on research, planning, and outlining before writing, but I often found myself writing my papers only a night or two before they were due. When I finally realized the importance of writing drafts in advance to allow my mind to work through the ideas and discover new ones, and to allow feedback from professors and my peers whom I asked to read my work, a great deal of the anxiety related to paper writing disappeared. Because I allowed myself time to think, I became more and more confident that I was turning in pieces of quality work.
>
> —Ross Wilken, Writing Assistant at
> Dartmouth University

Online Writing Centers

Some schools are introducing writing help on the Internet. You can e-mail your essay to the writing center and get responses, but it will probably take longer than a face-to-face meeting.

syndactyly: having webbed toes or fingers

Strategy 2: Read Out Loud

I always read my paper aloud to myself, pretending I am addressing an audience. When something sounds ridiculous, I can just see
someone objecting.

—Mia Hughes, Davidson College

In the words of an immortal Sesame Street song, "Don't worry if it's not good
enough for anyone else to hear." We know it's embarrassing, but we're concerned
with the quality of your paper, not popularity with your roommates. We don't know
what you're concerned with, but we're writing this book and what we say goes.

Reading out loud allows you to evaluate how conversational your writing is, and
it allows you to analyze how well the paper flows and how much sense it makes.
Muttering aloud not only helps the revising process, but also the drafting process, just so you know.

The act of reading aloud gives the writer more objectivity, too.
Listening to the work allows the writer to react to the sound of the
words and sentences and ideas; most students pick out their own
irregularities, ambivalences, and awkwardnesses.

—Charlotte Weiss Perlin, Writing Center
Director, University of Miami

Read it aloud. Especially if you are tired, you will notice awkward
sentences or typos that you would miss if you read silently. If your
roommates think you are going insane, console yourself with the
fact you'll get a better grade.

—Kelly Flannery-Reilly, Princeton University

Of all the good rules for improving your writing, the best one is this:
When you THINK you have a good final draft, print it out (on scrap
paper, if you have any) and then, pen in hand, read it aloud, either
to a friend or to yourself. LISTEN to it, listen closely. Enter your
many improvements and then, if you have time, do it again, this

time with a friend reading it aloud to you. What was a possible 'B+'
paper will by now have become at least an 'A–.'

> —Wayne C. Booth, George M. Pullman
> Distinguished Service Professor
> Emeritus in English Language and
> Literature, University of Chicago

Strategy 3: Print It Out

Papers look entirely different on your computer screen from how they appear
printed out. It's a scientific fact. Ask any self-respecting scientist; they study this
sort of thing. Besides, you can't get e-mail or play Freecell on a hard copy.

> If I could teach the students in my freshman writing class only one
> thing, it would be to print out each essay, read from the hard copy,
> preferably aloud, and then make any necessary changes before
> submitting the paper. For some reason, it is almost impossible to
> convince them of the necessity of this simple step. Students make
> innumerable excuses ("I don't have a printer in my room; I feel like
> a dork reading aloud; I didn't have time.") but I am convinced that
> taking the extra half hour to do this would, in almost every case,
> make the difference between a C and a C+, or even a B+ and an A.
>
> —Maud McInerney, Department of English,
> Haverford College

> When I am done with my first draft, I print it out and go over it with
> a red pen, almost as if I were a professor. I look at it trying to see
> it from a professor's point of view and make as any changes as I
> think necessary. Then I go back to the computer and revise over it
> as many times as I think it needs it. Usually I will let it sit for a cou-
> ple of hours at least between revisions so that I have time for it to
> settle out of the front of my mind.
>
> —Cat Kizer, Davidson, biology major

tresayle: a grandfather's grandfather

Easy on the Eyes

According to the American Academy of Ophthalmology, while computer monitors are not actually harmful to your eyes, prolonged staring at a screen can result in eye-irritation, fatigue, and difficulty focusing, with the possibility of headaches and muscle spasms. Prevent these symptoms by keeping your monitor at a comfortable distance and level, but more importantly, by taking breaks from your computer. In other words, printing a hard copy of your paper is good for both your grade and your well-being.

Many students find that they're more in control of revision when they can physically mark up their papers. The change in scene (from fuzzy computer screen to recycled wood pulp) enables them to notice more of those little typos.

What helps separate you from your paper even more is to print out the paper in a different font, a different style, or with different spacing. This slight differentiation decreases the familiarity with the paper and helps you see a mistake that you've skimmed over five times already.

> Change the font or the size of the font. The late author Michael Dorris lectured on how this technique helped him see his writing differently, thus recognizing mistakes or shortcomings that he would not otherwise notice.
>
> —Kerry Flannery-Reilly, Princeton University

If you're planning on making significant revisions (which you should), it may be helpful to print your paper out in revising-friendly format at least the first time around.

- Temporarily triple-space your paper
- Make your margins really big so you can add comments or redraft sentences
- Leave extra spaces in between paragraphs that you can already identify as weak

• Make the font especially large so you can squeeze words into sentences easily

Strategy 4: Use a Cover Sheet

So let's assume you've considered #3 a brilliant idea and have dutifully printed out your paper. People who really want to ensure that they'll examine every word can use a cover sheet. Take a piece of paper and slide it down each line, reading each line individually. This too will change the appearance of the paper and prevent you from skipping over mistakes.

This technique is more appropriate for the proofreading step than for your editing process, but keep it in mind. (Read on to the end of this chapter for the difference between these steps.)

Strategy 5: Make a Postdraft Outline

> My favorite way to improve structure and ensure that my paper supports its thesis is to make an outline *after* the paper is written, based on the draft itself. I state the thesis, and put this idea at the top of the outline. Then I go through the paper, pulling out the main ideas and prime examples from each paragraph and use them to form the body of the outline. From there, I get a general idea of the paper's movement, and each idea's relevance becomes clear. I then leave what is good, move what is out of place and scrap what does not fit. I find this process to be the best way to really improve a paper; it enables a write to step back from her work, which allows for a more objective, and thus better, critic.
>
> —Leda Eizenberg, Dartmouth College
> Student Writing Assistant

Many professors recommend this strategy as a tool for identifying extraneous information. Since drafting by definition encourages you to jot down as much as you want, it's expected that there will be some repetition and overlap of information. Once you've formulated this postdraft outline, evaluate each sentence: Is it essential to the point? Does it make sense? Does it support the thesis?

triskaidekaphobia: fear of the number 13

EDITING AND PROOFREADING:

Because Revising Just Isn't Enough

Make Your Own Paper!

Don't steal from your school's computer lab when you can whip up a batch of your own. Here's how: Take old scraps of paper (with a minimum of ink) and rip them up until you have about a cup. The lint from clothes-dryer traps also makes good starting material, along with regular paper. Take a window screen and cut it to the desired size (building mainte-nance people love this!). Pulpify your paper scraps in a blender filled about three-quarters full (or one quarter empty) with water. Add the scraps slowly. Fill a tub with clean water and throw the blended scrap concoction into the tub. Swirl the water so the scraps are floating around, then dip your window screen into the tub. Let the scraps settle on the frame, then pull it out and cover it with a piece of felt. Apply pres-sure with a rolling pin to remove the water. Then hang to dry over your roommate's bed. Easy and fun!

Now that you're utterly convinced of revision's importance, what does it entail? So important is the revision process that experts have divided it into two cate-gories: editing and proofreading. The experts know everything, even where you live. And if you don't do what they say, be ready for them to pay you a little visit.

> The best writing works on a number of different levels, much like a medieval cathedral. The smallest carving (the grammar, the punc-tuation, the referencing) should be as well crafted as the whole structure (the argument, the rationale for writing about something in the first place, the insight that the piece brings to the reader). Students need to learn to think both in terms of the details that will support their arguments and in terms of the arguments which they will need details to support: The whole structure depends on the richness of detail which they bring to it, but without a structure, there is little point for detail. Likewise, the process of writing may be likened to the construction of such a cathedral: Medieval archi-tects (or masons) began with master plans, but the building itself

might have taken decades, even centuries to complete, by which time fashions and interests, or rather ideas about what was worth representing, might have radically changed, thus necessitating revisions to the original. Sometimes even when the structures were completed, the vaults collapsed, and the builders had to start all over again.

In other words, writing is a process of learning, of trying out techniques that may or may not work the first time, and it is fatal to expect soaring vaults without strong foundations (in other people's writing and thinking) and adequate materials (i.e., writing skills).

—Rachel Fulton, Professor, University of Chicago

Ed•it (v.t.) 1. a. To prepare (written material) for publication or presentation, as by correcting, revising, or adapting. b. To prepare an edition of for publication: edit a collection of short stories. c. To modify or adapt so as to make suitable or acceptable 2. To assemble the components of (a film or soundtrack, for example), as by cutting and splicing. 3. To eliminate; delete

Proof•read (v.t.) To read (copy or proof) in order to find errors and mark corrections.

What's the difference? Editing involves the larger issues: organization, arguments, transitions, and such. Proofreading, however, includes the more microscopic concerns like grammar and word choice.

Don't overwhelm yourself by doing one round of revision in which you look at every possible concern. Identify those areas where you're especially vulnerable to making mistakes. Maybe you too easily stray off on tangents. Maybe you always

truckle: a cylindrical or barrel-shaped cheese

mix up *effect* and *affect*. Maybe your topic sentences tend to be unclear. To do one read-through in which you try to locate each of those errors would be over-whelming, and most likely you'd miss some mistakes.

Knowing What to Look for

Obviously, if you were to go through every sentence checking for every possible grammatical problem, you probably wouldn't be able to hand your paper in until, roughly speaking, mid-September 2007. One of the keys to proofreading, therefore, is to figure out what grammatical problems you commonly make, then go through your paper looking for these particular problems.

Most likely you don't know what your common problems are—otherwise you wouldn't be making them anymore. Look through any old, graded papers from last semester and see if there's any kind of consistency in professor's comments. Go find the writing tutor and have him or her look over your work. Tutors are paid (with your tuition money) to help you figure out just these kind of problems. Use them.

Some people find it helpful to read through their papers multiple times with a single concern each time. During your first read-through, for example, you might be especially attentive to your topic sentences. As you read through a second time, you may look at only repetitive word choice.

Other students break each reading into two parts. The first time through, they'll mark everything that's wrong. The second time through, they'll correct each error.

Sure, you'll become increasingly sick of your paper after you've read through it 25 times, but the more you read through it, the more opportunity you'll have to discover mistakes and refine your writing. Overkill is an idea that's foreign to revision.

With that thought in mind, we've devoted the next two chapters to editing and proofreading.

Chapter Six	# EDITING

As we discussed in the first chapter, writing a paper requires both creative and critical energy. The editing stage demands critical energy. Start by examining the broad issues and gradually focus on more specific weaknesses. We'll lead you through the process in this chapter.

GENERAL EDITING CONCERNS

Here are some of the big questions to ask yourself as you read through your paper.

Does Your Thesis Still Work?

Begin editing where you began this whole writing endeavor: the thesis. It's worthwhile to reexamine some of the concerns you addressed when constructing the thesis. That the thesis has evolved as you've researched, organized, and written is not necessarily bad. In fact, an altered thesis reveals that you are truly considering how well your paper molds to your argument. Here are some questions you might consider to evaluate your thesis:

- How focused is the thesis? Are you truly arguing a particular side?
- How closely does the paper address this thesis? Is each facet of your thesis explained and argued sufficiently?

- Should the thesis be amended to more accurately convey the direction your paper has taken, or should the structure and contents of your paragraphs be altered to more closely align with your thesis?
- Can your analysis be extended further?
- Can you think of any changes that might make your thesis more convincing?
- Have you approached but not developed the author's argument?

I like to think of a paper like a mathematical proof (just think of high school geometry). A good paper proves its point because the reader never has an opportunity to question the writer's logic.

—Andrew Berglund, Writing Tutor,
Dartmouth University

How Will It Sound to Others?

Consider the overall tone of your paper. Since different genres of academic writing address different audiences with various concerns, you should examine how well your paper addresses your particular audience.

Write as if you are talking to your grandmother.

—Dr. Rebecca Petersen,
clinical psychologist

- Is the tone appropriate for the intended audience?
- Have you addressed some of the concerns that this particular audience may raise?
- Have you given a sufficient summary that equips the reader with the background information that is necessary to an understanding of your argument, or
- Have you lapsed into the summary trap and neglected the argument?
- Have you offered an objective, factual argument, or has your personal opinion inhibited an honest evaluation of the evidence?

rakehell: an utterly debauched person

Take a moment to think about the structure of your paper. If you made an outline in the prewriting process, ask yourself if your paper adheres to the outline. Does your evidence support your thesis? Is the order of your examples logical? If you did not make an outline, try to envision what an outline for your paper would look like. If you can't see how you would categorize your examples or how your conclusion builds on your thesis and evidence, consider making changes.

—Kerry Flannery-Reilly, Princeton
University

Perspective taking involves continually putting oneself in the reader's perspective and not availing that perspective of all the unspoken assumptions and unspoken ideas we utilized while writing. "How might this come across?" is often more important than "Did I say what I meant to say?" Considering alternative ways it may come across is key as well. Providing one's projected reader pointers and trail markers can better focus us on what we need to say and how.

—Bill Puka, Professor of Philosophy and
Psychology, Rensselaer Polytechnic
Institute

Have You Considered Other Viewpoints?

Consider the counterarguments. To ignore opposing viewpoints can discredit your thesis, since many will assume that you have not given the topic enough thought or that you are unable to challenge it and dispute it.

- Have you examined possible objections that a critical reader would raise?
- How well have you defended your thesis against such counterarguments?
- Have you informed the reader *why* your argument withstands the potential counterarguments?

Writing As Dialogue

Generating different angles on an idea is especially important when one "can't think of more to say" about a topic. "If someone disagreed with the main points I've put forward here, how might they do so? How might the same point be made in totally different terms? What sorts of highly credible ideas in another area can be used as analogues to what I'm saying? Suppose a supportive observer wished to celebrate my point: What sorts of support might she or he rally for them, what sorts of added significance might he or she discern, what unexpected or otherwise valuable implications from them might she draw? How might I pre-empt or reply to possible criticisms? How might I accommodate them, posing remedies to my views if the flaws and limitations pointed out prove credible?" These are good questions to ask.

—Bill Puka, Professor of Philosophy and
Psychology, Rennsselaer Polytechnic
Institute

As far as argumentative writing goes, I most like student writing (or any critical writing) that anticipates objections and tries to meet them fairly. So when students come to me and say: "I've written a draft of my paper, and it's 20 percent shorter than it should be, and I don't know how to extend it," I usually advise them to imagine what kind of questions might be raised about the argument by the student in the class whose comments they most respect, or to recall what evidence they have had to exclude in the act of making the argument in the first place. The last part of the paper can then be profitably used to discuss such problems, if not to solve them. I remind them that when they themselves are reading, nothing is probably more persuasive than finding themselves thinking "yes, but..." and then seeing the author addressing their own reservations in the next paragraph. The ancient model for this kind of "proleptic" writing is the *Phaedrus,* which concerns the invention of writing itself, and where Plato offers his clearest defense of why he writes in dialogue form.

—James Chandler, George M. Pullman
Professor of English, University of Chicago

woopknacker: an aggressive loud-mouthed person

Too Long? Too Short? Just Right?

Consider the length of the paper. Most professors enforce the guidelines they have provided. In fact, some professors will penalize a paper that has not conformed to the assigned length. Remember that your professor probably will not enjoy reading the paper that's three times the proscribed length. If an assignment gives a range of pages (i.e., 10–15), aim at the lower limit. This aim should not be out of laziness, but rather out of a desire to be as succinct as possible. Sometimes the paper is longer not out of necessity but out of a lack of understanding. Rambling sentences might hint that you do not have a clear grasp of your topic.

- Have you met or exceeded the necessary page requirement?
- What areas could use additional evidence?
- What areas may not need to be as closely scrutinized?
- Should the introduction and/or conclusion be expanded or condensed?
- Given page constraints, could the paper go more in depth?
- Has an overly detailed, deep analysis of one argument forced you to neglect other facets of your thesis?
- Is your paper too deep for the assignment?

Having examined some of the broad questions, you are ready to concentrate on more specific areas. Specific editing concerns may be loosely assigned to two categories: 1) coherence and clarity, and 2) conciseness.

COHERENCE AND CLARITY
(or If It's Not Lucid You Better Not Use It)

Coherent papers will eliminate choppy sentences and provide transitions to make the arguments flow. These transitions will conflate separate arguments and allow you to build one idea on top of another. How can you create a conversational flow in your essay? Employ repeated words or synonyms, apply transitional statements, and consider sentence structure.

> Word carpentry is like any other kind of carpentry: You must join your sentences smoothly.
>
> —Anatole France

Ezra Pound wrote that the truest test of sincerity is craft, which is itself a word for informed attention, selection, retrospection, and a willingness to tear the whole house down to get the windows right. I think any student who has something he or she believes should be heard would do well to ask what techniques are available in that genre (essay, poem, story). I don't think it's possible to overemphasize the value of economy, precision, and coherence. Practice based on these considerations can lead to the development of a serviceable style, and of course, Flaubert says the end of all style is clarity. It's wonderful to be evocative and complex and useful, but clarity has to precede these.

—Rod T. Smith, Professor, Washington
and Lee University, editor of
Shenandoah

Repeated Terms and Phrases

Keep your reader on track. If the reader gets lost, you will not be there to explain, "This is what I was referring to—remember the last paragraph?" Save your reader the effort and frustration by using recurring terms.

> The advantage of small **dogs** stems mainly from their ability to fit into **handbaskets**. Dorothy did not own a giant Schnauzer because smaller **"handbasket dogs"** fit more easily into the pocket on long yellow-brick-road treks.

As important as it is to be perfectly clear for your reader, constant repetition will put him to sleep. Stylistic and lucid writing will diversify words while still reminding the reader what you're discussing. Here's where the thesaurus comes in handy. Before rushing to this valuable reference, creatively explore all the synonyms you can list. If you've come to a blank, however, check out the related words that the thesaurus suggests.

kakamora: fabled supernatural fairies who fear anything white

> The **tranquilizing** effect of the **poppy field sedated** Dorothy and her companions until, **soporific** from the **pacifying opiates**, they collapsed, **sleeping** amongst the **narcotic flowers**.

Don't restrict yourself to exact synonyms. Another means of varying your words while guiding your reader is to substitute short, descriptive phrases for the words you want to repeat.

> *The Wizard of Oz* portrays the **munchkins** as domineering when they are assembled en masse; **the entire community of dwarfs** demanded that Dorothy "Follow the yellow brick road." Terrified, she had no choice but to obey the **vertically challenged throng**.

Another way of guiding your reader through your paragraph is to substitute pronouns for previously mentioned words. Use pronouns sparingly, however. If too many nondescript *he, she,* or *it* words creep into your paragraph, your reader may get confused.

Which is easier to follow?

> **Munchkins** like lollipops; **they** appointed a Lollipop Guild to distribute **them**.

Or

> **Munchkins** like lollipops; **they** appointed a Lollipop Guild to distribute these **sweet treats**.

> When writing a paper, it's important to retain a sense of motion. The reader should be pulled along and released all the time, like in novels or in good songs. This tension and release will retain the reader's interest. And don't forget to make the whole essay move forward all the while.
>
> —Sarah Ingram, Amherst College, music major

Transitions

Good writing incorporates two types of transitions. First, it will have transitions that connect sentences and make the writing flow. Varying sentence structure and inserting transition words will not only guide your reader, but it will also eliminate choppiness by creating a conversational tone.

The second type of transition will connect entire paragraphs and ideas with one another. Clear papers navigate your reader from point to point by utilizing transition words and phrases. It's as if you're giving directions to Lamar Higgins, who doesn't have a map or, quite frankly, a full deck. You want to tell him to turn right at the McDonalds, go a couple feet past the old oak tree, turn right when he sees the red mailbox, and go up the little hill over the pleasant crick and down the lane past Farmer Smith's brick house. Leave out a step, and our hero Lamar will end up at a llama farm in Brazil.

Likewise, you as the writer must constantly give directions that indicate to the reader how you're getting to your final point. You must provide noteworthy landmarks that clue your reader in, informing him of the direction you're taking. The most basic of your paper's directions comes in the form of transitional words or phrases, linking the parts of a sentence. More advanced transitions will connect entire ideas.

> First, the introduction makes a clear and reasonable claim. Then each sentence follows logically from the one before, always with the goal of bringing the reader nearer to the writer's conclusion. The same goes for paragraphs, chapters, sections, and volumes. If each one follows from the one before, and logically flows into the next, then the reader never has a chance to disagree. By making sure the reader is there for every step, then the reader must be there at the end of the race!
>
> —Andrew Berglund, writing tutor,
> Dartmouth University

siffleur: a professional whistler

Transitional Words

Make sure your paper uses words like the following to help keep the reader on track.

Sequence
again, also, and, and then, besides, finally, first...second...third, following, in addition, furthermore, last, moreover, next, still, too

> **Following** the signing of Treaty of Paris, the politicians played an intense game of Risk.

Time
after a bit, after a few days, after a while, afterward, as long as, as soon as, at last, at length, at that time, before, earlier, immediately, in the meantime, in the past, lately, later, meanwhile, now, presently, shortly, simultaneously, since, so far, soon, then, thereafter, until, when

> **Before** someone discovered his talent as a clown, Biggles had never even considered joining the circus.

Comparison
again, also, in the same way, just as, likewise, once more, similarly

> **Just as** M & M candies "melt in your mouth and not in your hand," **so also** do the delectable Reese's Pieces get eaten before their orange, brown, and yellow shells can stain your palm.

Contrast
although, but, despite, even though, however, in contrast, in spite of, instead, nevertheless, nonetheless, notwithstanding, on the contrary, on the one hand . . . on the other hand, regardless, still, though, yet

> **Even though** the student cried vigorously, the professor would not change her grade on the paper. "Cry me a river," he chastised, "Tears will never mend the wrongs of choppy writing. **Despite** your emotions, I cannot change your grade."

Examples

after all, even, for example, for instance, indeed, in fact, of course, specifically, such as, the following example, to illustrate

> Kentucky officials have failed to eliminate stupid laws. **In fact,** it is still illegal to transport ice cream in your pocket in Lexington.

Cause and Effect

accordingly, as a result, because, consequently, for this purpose, hence, so, then, therefore, thereupon, thus, to this end

> In Wyoming, it is illegal to take a picture of a rabbit in the month of June. Professional photographers, **therefore,** schedule their photo shoots later in the summer.

Place

above, adjacent to, below, beyond, closer to, elsewhere, far, farther on, here, near, nearby, opposite to, there, to the left, to the right

> The Continental Divide marks the spot in which the water of America flows in opposite directions. **Below** this spot lies the most beautiful landscape I've ever seen.

Concession

although it is true that, granted that, I admit that, it may appear that, naturally, of course, while

> **While** it might appear that people are no longer superstitious, doctors report that some of their patients suffer from *triskadecaphobia* (the fear of the number 13).

Summary, Repetition, or Conclusion:

as a result, as has been noted, as I have said, as we have seen, as mentioned earlier, in any event, in conclusion, in other words, in short, on the whole, therefore, to summarize

> **philtrum:** the indentation that divides the upper lip

The paper is due tomorrow. **In other words,** you will not be getting any sleep tonight.

When these transition words are used improperly, however, they can actually detract from your writing. Adding a transition phrase to coerce a paragraph into a place where it doesn't belong will not work. You can identify such an error by common sense. Does the transition word seem awkward or contrived? It's probably out of place.

Bad Transition
Cookies and cream is a really good ice cream flavor. **Moreover,** pistachio is gross.

When using transition words or phrases, you should also make sure they don't observe the obvious or abuse hollow and general clichés. Offending or boring your reader by making pointless and pontifical statements is not advised. In addition to the problem of misusing transition phrases, watch out for transition phrases that invite pontification or vagueness. Some dangerous transition words include:

> *Therefore, it's clear that*
> *It is important to observe that*
> *Clearly, this is true because*
> *It should be apparent that*

It is important to note that these statements are not always inappropriate in an academic essay (or in *The Yale Daily News Guide to Writing College Papers,* for that matter). If you explain why "it is important to note," for example, and if you avoid constant use of such generalizations, these transitional phrases can be effective.

Winners of the "Worst Analogies Ever Written in a High School Essay" Contest

He spoke with the wisdom that can only come from experience, like a guy who went blind because he looked at a solar eclipse without one of those boxes with a pinhole in it and now goes around the country speaking at high schools about the dangers of looking at a solar eclipse without one of those boxes with a pinhole in it.

She caught your eye like one of those pointy hook latches that used to dangle from screen doors and would fly up whenever you banged the door open again.

The little boat gently drifted across the pond exactly the way a bowling ball wouldn't.

McBride fell 12 stories, hitting the pavement like a Hefty Bag filled with vegetable soup.

From the attic came an unearthly howl. The whole scene had an eerie, surreal quality, like when you're on vacation in another city and *Jeopardy* comes on at 7 P.M. instead of 7:30.

Her hair glistened in the rain like nose hair after a sneeze.

Her eyes were like two brown circles with big black dots in the center.

Bob was as perplexed as a hacker who means to access T:flw.quid55328.com\aaakk/ch@ung but gets T:\flw.quidaaakk/ch@ung by mistake.

Her vocabulary was as bad as, like, whatever.

He was as tall as a six-foot-three-inch tree.

The hailstones leaped from the pavement, just like maggots when you fry them in hot grease.

borbgorble: to wander about aimlessly

Her date was pleasant enough, but she knew that if her life was a movie this guy would be buried in the credits as something like "Second Tall Man."

Long separated by cruel fate, the star-crossed lovers raced across the grassy field toward each other like two freight trains, one having left Cleveland at 6:36 P.M. traveling at 55 mph, the other from Topeka at 4:19 P.M. at a speed of 35 mph.

The politician was gone but unnoticed, like the period after the Dr. on a Dr Pepper can.

They lived in a typical suburban neighborhood with picket fences that resembled Nancy Kerrigan's teeth.

John and Mary had never met. They were like two hummingbirds who had also never met.

The thunder was ominous-sounding, much like the sound of a thin sheet of metal being shaken backstage during the storm scene in a play.

His thoughts tumbled in his head, making and breaking alliances like underpants in a dryer without Cling Free.

The red brick wall was the color of a brick-red Crayola crayon.

Creative Punctuation

Your parents, your elementary school teacher, your middle school teacher, and your high school teacher have all tried to acquaint you with the basic tenets of English grammar. College is where you show that you not only know how to apply all those nitpicky rules, but also that you can practice them creatively.

Don't always limit yourself to boring commas and periods: Learn to use the vibrant, go-getting colon. Don't shy away from using a dash—even two—in your essay. Join two short sentences with a semicolon;

> My mother's menu consisted of two choices: Take it or leave it.
>
> —Buddy Hackett

it will help the flow of your paper. Why not ask a question? Although the complexities of the English language have resulted in extensive grammar standards, punctuation was invented not to burden the writer, but rather to equip him with an opportunity to more clearly express his thoughts.

> Students should be more willing to use all forms of punctuation—including dashes, semicolons, colons.
>
> —Thomas Gustafson, Associate Professor of English, University of Southern California

> Rather than break up their ideas into digestible bite-sized sentences, many students like to use lots of commas in sentences in a stream-of-consciousness manner with the result that sentences become long and unwieldy. This kind of writing makes the reader (and teacher) work too hard. Students seem to have trouble with the correct use of words like *but* and *however* which separate contrasting ideas, not similar ideas.
>
> —Michael Lane, Professor of Journalism and Public Information at Emerson University

If you've never learned how to use punctuation, look at a grammar book or an Internet site. We scavenged around and found some especially helpful sites that you can use gratis.

Books

William Strunk Jr.'s *Elements of Style*
Richard A. Lanham's *Revising Prose*

Internet Sites

http://www.bartleby.com/141/index.html

> I believe in getting into hot water; it keeps you clean.
>
> —G. K. Chesterton

Daily Grammar is a site that will send you a grammar lesson every day. http://www.dailygrammar.com

fernticled: covered with freckles

This is a site that is pretty comprehensive.
http://papyr.com/hypertextbooks/engl_126/book126.htm

Okay, so it's a British site, and they use words like *parlour* and *splendiferous*. But those Brits do know a thing or two (or many, as this site evidences) about grammar.
http://www.edunet.com/english/grammar/index.cfm

Active Versus Passive Voice

Using the active voice is another way to write more clearly. Passive voice can confuse a sentence by making it more ambiguous, less direct, and less strong. How can a sentence in the passive voice be identified? The verb "to be" *(am, is, are, was, were, be, being, been)* often indicates that you're using passive voice.

When writing academic papers, students seem especially prone to lapse into passive writing. Michael Lane, Professor of Public Information at Emerson University explains this concept and its remedy:

> Many students like to write in the passive voice. Rather than write "the man shot the cop," they would rather write "shots were fired." This leads to confused writing, ambiguity, and overall fuzziness. The reader doesn't know who is taking what action. "Votes were cast," "it is generally believed," "there was negativity in this past political campaign," are the kind of sentences some students like to write without tying the action or assertions to anyone in particular.

Passive
The gloves were worn by O. J.

Active
O. J. wore the gloves.

Passive
Donald Duck cartoons were banned in Finland because pants were not worn routinely by the Disney character.

Active
The government of Finland banned Donald Duck cartoons because the Disney character routinely refused to wear pants.

Passive voice is not *always* a major violation of writing code; about three percent of the time, passive voice can be used constructively. (We'll assume one of those instances was the last sentence.) Passive voice is acceptable if:

- The subject or agent is unknown or inconsequential.

Example
The meeting time was changed from 7:00 to 8:00.

- The object being acted upon needs to be emphasized.

Example
The annoying buzz of the fly was silenced by the sudden sweep of the fly-swatter.

- The agent can be more effectively modified if it is placed at the end of a sentence.

Example
The silence of the dawn **was interrupted** by the shrill sirens of the fire alarm that awoke the students from their peaceful slumber.

- The paper is scientific.

Example
In this experiment, the compound tetraphenylphthalic anhydride was synthesized through a four-step procedure, beginning with the starting materials benzil, or 1,2-diphenyl-1,2-ethanedione, and dibenzylketone, or 1,3-diphenyl-2-propanone.

hystricine: having to do with porcupines

Sexist Language

Even if your professor is not a femi-Nazi, you should learn to use gender-neutral language. Even though using *he* or *man* is grammatically correct, some professors will tell you that using masculine words like *man* or *him* to apply to generic or universal statements is no longer acceptable in academic writing. If you're writing about Elvis, feel free to use *man* or *him* or *his*. If you're writing without a specific subject, however, you should be wary of sexist language.

Sometimes you'll see writers use feminine pronouns simply to avoid accusations of chauvinism. You'll see statements like, "A good professor will make herself available to her students," or "A geophysicist must keep her data as organized as possible." It's better to be completely gender-neutral.

Listed below are some common areas in which sexist language may surface.

General

Biased	Neutral
mankind	humanity, people, human beings
the best man for the job	the best person for the job
the common man	the average person, ordinary people
workman	worker

Occupations

Biased	Neutral
chairman	coordinator, head, chair
businessman	business executive
fireman	firefighter
mailman	mail carrier
policeman	police officer
congressman	congressional representative

Pronouns

Here are some tricks to erasing any gender-specific pronouns.

Make your pronouns plural. While English separates the singular into female and male (*his* or *her*), the plural applies to both genders (*their*).

Biased

The wombat understands who **his** predators are—Investment bankers who drive expensive Jaguars.

Neutral

Wombats understand who their predators are—Mary Kay salespeople who wear too much makeup.

Reword to avoid any controversy. Here's an example of a sentence that's been rewritten to sidestep an offensive pronoun.

Biased

The average wombat worries that **he** will be stepped on by an expensive wing-tip.

Neutral

The average wombat worries about a confrontation with a light pink Cadillac.

Replace the masculine pronoun with one, you, *or (sparingly)* he or she, *as appropriate.* While this tactic allows you to skirt the gender issue (no pun intended), using these words can make your writing seem unnecessarily abstract or convoluted.

Biased

The wombat who emerges victorious after an arm-wrestling match with Lieutenant Dan from *Forrest Gump* will be satisfied with **his** strength and wit.

Neutral

The wombat who emerges victorious after consuming a box of chocolate will

---

splanohnic: a gut feeling

be satisfied with **his** or **her** strength and wit.

Biased

He who leaves unwrapped Twinkies on his doorstep saves the life of a wombat.

Neutral

One who buys stock in the Hostess corporation saves the life of a wombat.

Watch out for indefinite pronouns. By definition, indefinite pronouns are, well, indefinite. Words like *everybody, everyone, anybody,* or *anyone* invite gender specific language. If you apply the rules above to these instances, however, you should be okay.

Biased

Anyone who belongs to the "Support a Wombat" club must pay **his** dues by Wednesday.

Neutral

Anyone who belongs to the "Support a Wombat" club must pay dues by Wednesday.

Neutral

Members of the "Support a Wombat" club must pay their dues by Wednesday.

Neutral

Anyone who belongs to the "Support a Wombat" club must pay **his or her** dues by Wednesday.

Use first- or second-person perspective. Only the third person requires gender specification. Using first- or second-person pronouns, however, might not be acceptable for all types of papers.

Biased

The wombat admirer will go to the zoo, wear **his** "I love wombats" badge, and observe wombat behavior for hours.

Neutral

I, a wombat admirer, go to the zoo, wear **my** "I love wombats" badge, and observe wombat behavior for hours.

Use an article instead of a possessive pronoun as a modifier.

Biased
When the wombat goes back into **his** cage to read today's *Wall Street Journal*, **his** admirers weep and leave.

Neutral
When the wombat goes back into the cage to read yesterday's *Bloom County Comics*, the admirers weep and leave.

Use the passive voice. This solution should be applied sparingly, since we've already discussed why the active voice is preferable.

Biased
If a wombat wishes to avoid sex bias in **his** writing, **he** should examine these alternatives.

Neutral
These alternatives should be examined by any wombat who wishes to avoid sex bias.

THINK POSITIVE!

Expressing statements in the positive also can make your writing more clear. Positive statements are preferable to negative statements since affirmative statements tend to be more direct and concise than their negative alternatives. Why? Williams Zinssler, author of *Writing Well*, explains, "To understand the negative, we have to translate it into an affirmative, because the negative only implies what we should do by telling us what we shouldn't do. The affirmative states it directly."

Look at how much more condensed the following examples are:

gelogenic: inducing laughter

Don't break my heart, my achy, breaky heart.
versus
Be nice.

Don't turn around, you're not welcome anymore.
versus
Leave.

No, I don't want your number, and no, I don't really want to give you mine.
versus
Stop harassing me.

Before we lose any more credibility ("What are these authors suggesting? Those lyrics happen to be an art form!"), let us qualify our examples. Sometimes the longer, negative phrases are more appropriate: They can be descriptive, emphatic, and articulate. If you intend to be as concise as possible on a point that need not be emphasized, eliminating the negative might be beneficial. If you want to accentuate a contradiction or an antithesis, eliminating the negative might not be effective.

"Ask not what your country can do for you, ask what you can do for your country."

"Don't walk—run to the library nearest you."

"Never fear, Superman is here."

CONCISENESS (or If in Doubt, Toss It Out)

> Students need to focus on tightening their sentences and paragraphs. Clear and direct writing seems to be a lost art. As one of my professors once told me, "every word in the essay should be important—if you eliminate a word and it doesn't make a difference, then you didn't need it in the first place.
>
> —Christina Gómez, Professor of Sociology
> and Latin American, Latino, and
> Caribbean Studies, Dartmouth College

So maybe you're the kid who's always adjusting the margins, enlarging the font, and messing with the spacing to somehow meet that 15-page mark. Perhaps you should more thoroughly research or develop your ideas. Or, perhaps you're that student who might be able to get 15 pages if the text were put into size 7, single spaced, with 1/8 inch margins. Eliminating superfluous words, phrases, and even sections of your paper will be the most important editing task. Remember, the Gettysburg Address was only 267 words. Authors struggle with the elimination of words and chapters and sentences all the time.

The key to conciseness is being willing to acknowledge that some words are, well, trash. Just as that big plastic bag overflowing with old pizza boxes and aluminum cans (*Recycle! Recycle!*) that's been sitting in the corner of your room for a couple weeks is gross, so also is the paper that still has excess words, ideas, and paragraphs.

> If you would be pungent, be brief; for it is with words as well as sunbeams—the more they are condensed, the deeper they burn.
>
> —Robert Southey

> Writers have two main problems. One is writer's block, when the words won't come at all, and the other is logorrhea, when the words come so fast that they can hardly get to the wastebasket in time.
> —Ceclia Bartholomew

The most effective writing will be condensed. Ernest Hemingway, when challenged to write a short story in as few words as possible, composed a six-word story: "For sale. Baby shoes. Never worn."

The key to condensed writing is abandoning your pride. You may think that you've completed the most masterful sentence ever to grace a piece of paper, but according to Thomas Wolfe, author of *Of Time and the River,* "The very bitter lesson that everyone who wants to write has got to learn, is that a thing may in itself be the finest piece of writing anyone has ever done, and yet have absolutely no place in the manuscript one hopes to publish."

cartophily: the collecting of bubble gum cards depicting famous people

Be Brief

To do a novel like one of mine, you have to write 80,000 pages in order to get 800.

> —Louis-Ferdinand Celine, *Journey to the End of the Night*

Brevity is the soul of wit.

> —William Shakespeare

The shorter and plainer the better.

> —Beatrix Potter

Let your words be few.

> —Ecclesiastes 5:2

The beautiful part of writing is that you don't have to get it right the first time, unlike, say, a brain surgeon. You can always do it better, find the exact word, the apt phrase, the leaping simile.

> —Robert Cormier

It is perfectly okay to write garbage—as long as you edit brilliantly.

> —C. J. Cherryh

Some Quick Tips on Eliminating Words

1. Imagine you're writing a classified ad in which you're charged by the word.

2. Pretend you are writing a column in which the length limit is one-third your current length. What *you* don't cut, your editor will.

3. Edit carefully so that nothing is repeated or said twice.

4. Remember that the attention spans of many readers were developed watching *Sesame Street*. Sure, your professor has more patience than most, but after reading 50 papers that say the exact same thing yours says, she probably won't appreciate the "fluff" you've included.

5. Remember that half the words have twice the impact.

Eliminate "Weasel Words"

Theodore Roosevelt coined this term because "the weasel sucks the heart out of an egg and leaves nothing but the empty shell." Below are some such "weasel words" and possible substitutions.

> • *the reason for, for the reason that, due to the fact that, owing to the fact that, in light of the fact that, considering the fact that, on the grounds that, this is why*
> ⇨*because, since, why*

> • *despite the fact that, regardless of the fact that, notwithstanding the fact that*
> ⇨*although, even though*

> • *in the event that, if it should transpire/happen that, under circumstances in which*
> ⇨*if*

> • *on the occasion of, in a situation in which, under circumstances in which*
> ⇨*when*

ombrosalgia: aches and pains when it rains

- *as regards, in reference to, with regard to concerning the matter of, where . . . is concerned*

⇨*about*

- *it is crucial that, it is necessary that, there is a need/necessity for, it is important that, it is incumbent upon, cannot be avoided*

⇨*must, should*

- *is able to, has the opportunity to, is in a position to, has the capacity for, has the ability to,*

⇨*can*

- *it is possible that, there is a chance that*

⇨*may, might*

- *it could happen that, the possibility exists for*

⇨*can, could*

- *prior to, in anticipation of, subsequent to, following on, at the same time as, simultaneously with*

⇨*before, after, as*

(This list comes from Joseph Williams, *Style: Ten Lessons in Clarity and Grace,* 4th ed. New York: HarperCollins College Publishers, 1994.)

Eliminate Redundant Words

Padding your writing with extra adjectives won't make your paper any more forceful; in fact, the fewer words you use, the more convincing you will be. Redundancies make you look dumb.

Example
Future plans. As compared to?
Unexpected surprise. Best kind.

> In writing anything, do whatever it takes to avoid the obvious. Nothing stinks like the obvious. If you aren't sure what the obvious is, consider the views of your parents on the subject at hand.
>
> —James Kincaid, Aerol Arnold Professor of
> English, University of Southern California

Some words are not necessarily redundant, but their inclusion offers no extra meaning. Some words that fall under this category include *very, somewhat, rather, slightly, sort of, kind of, extremely, absolutely.* Think about it: Does *totally absolute* make anything any more absolute? If not, cross the word out.

~~Rather~~ interesting ⇨ interesting

~~Completely~~ wrong ⇨ wrong

Reduce Wordy Verbs

is aware, has knowledge of ⇨ knows
is taking ⇨ takes
takes offense to ⇨ objects
gets mad at ⇨ disputes
are indications ⇨ indicate
are suggestive ⇨ suggest
doesn't get it ⇨ misunderstands

pogonotomy: a beard-growing contest

Chapter Seven — **PROOFREADING**

While having terrific organization and a focused, flowing paper is vital, it's important not to forget all the little things you learned way back in sixth grade. Each sentence needs to be as finely crafted as the overall paragraph.

When Ernest Hemingway was asked how much revising went into his books, he responded, "It depends. I rewrote the ending of *Farewell to Arms,* the last page of it, thirty-nine times before I was satisfied."

The reason for thirty-nine rewrites? "Getting the words right."

Hemingway did all right for himself, and you can too.

> Many college students have not yet mastered the rules of style that can be found in part one of Strunk and White's *Elements of Style.* "Get the little book," remains good advice.
> —Murray Dry, Professor of Law,
> Middlebury College

WORD CHOICE

> Everything should be made as simple as possible, but not simpler.
> —Albert Einstein

Had Einstein not been able to clearly convey $e = mc^2$ to his fellow research geniuses, no one would know about his work today. Likewise, your professors will not be able to identify the brilliance of your ideas unless you can clearly communicate them in your writing. It doesn't hurt to have long, unkempt, gray hair either.

> The difference between the right word and the almost right word is the difference between lightning and a lightning bug.
>
> —Mark Twain

Word choice is probably the greatest factor in clear writing. Therefore, choose your words with the utmost consideration and care. This choice will be difficult, especially since the English language boasts over one million words, giving English speakers the largest lexicon in the world. The following considerations will make this choice easier, however.

> If you simplify your English, you are freed from the worst follies of orthodoxy . . . One cannot change this all in a moment, but one can at least change one's own habits, and from time to time one can even, if one jeers loudly enough, send some worn-out and useless phrase . . . into the dustbin where it belongs.
>
> —George Orwell

Avoid Overdone Language

Don't let your ideas and arguments get entangled in pretentious language. Flexing your vocabulary brawn will not produce a more sophisticated paper. Eloquent verbiage will not cover up the obvious lack of insight in an essay. In fact, your erudite diction might lead your professor to empathize with the frustrations of Boris Pasternak, author of *Doctor Zhivago*: "Oh, how one wishes sometimes to escape from the meaningless dullness of human eloquence, from all those sublime phrases, to take refuge in nature, apparently so inarticulate, or in the wordlessness of long, grinding labor, of sound sleep, of true music, or of a human understanding rendered speechless by emotion!"

dwalm: a fainting spell

And we wouldn't want *that* to happen. We've never actually read *Doctor Zhivago*; heck, we haven't even watched the movie. But we're sure something nasty happens.

An ill-chosen word is the fool's messenger.

—Anonymous

Ernest Hemingway began his career in journalism where he learned to write with active verbs, short sentences, short paragraphs, and clarity. Later he described these techniques: "Those were the best rules I ever learned for the business of writing. I've never forgotten them." Professors and students agree that word choice and simplicity are essential.

Read through your paper, identifying words that people might perceive as "pompous prose"—words like the ones below. Or let's say you come across a word like *capricious*. Ask yourself some questions.

What If an Educator Had Written the Lord's Prayer?

Our Father-figure who resides in the upper-echelon domain,

May Thy title always be structured to elicit a favorable response.

Reward us today, bread-wise,

Our Father-figure who resides in the upper-echelon domain,

May Thy title always be structured to elicit a favorable response.

Reward us today, bread-wise,

And minimize our unfavorable self-concept, resulting from credit overextension,

As we will strive to practice reciprocal procedures.

And channel us, not into temptation-inducing areas,

But provide us with security from situations not conducive to moral enrichment.

For Thine is the position of maximum achievement in the power structure,

Not to mention the prestige-attainment factor that never terminates.

Amen.

—Tom Dodge, in *English Journal*, January, 1971

1. Do you know what *capricious* means?

2. Does your reader know what *capricious* means? (Remember your audience: If you're writing a children's book, this might not be the most sagacious jargon to adopt. If it's your professor, chances are that he's learned it sometime during high school, in his undergrad work, his graduate school, in research for his Ph.D., etcetera.)

3. Is this word necessary? Does it *really* help communicate your idea, or are you just looking for an excuse to show your professor that you can use college-sized words?

4. Would eliminating this word be productive? Big words were invented for a reason: They describe ideas. If you removed this word, would you have to spend ten words describing the idea it represented?

5. Does this word keep the sentence clear? Clarity in writing is more valuable than erudition. Professors grade content with more scrutiny than they do for vocabulary prowess.

> One great use of words is to hide our thoughts.
>
> —Voltaire

> The safest words are those which bring us most directly to the facts.
>
> —William Shakespeare

> I think the casual tone of personal writing is what has helped me. I've learned that this can be applied to formal papers. While it is important to maintain a sophisticated and mature style when composing for classes, it's also important to "speak" to your readers. I think that keeping this in mind when writing and revising can significantly improve a paper.
>
> —Julia Henneberry, Dartmouth University

> Clutter is the disease of American writing. We are a society strangling in unnecessary words, circular constructions, pompous frills and meaningless jargon.
>
> —William Zinsser, *On Writing Well*

nuzzer: a ceremonial present

Eschew Obfuscation

While beautiful prose is certainly a wonderful stylistic plus to any paper, it is useless if the organization and argument of the paper is lost in beautiful but meaningless phrasing.

—Rita Mitchell, Dartmouth College
Writing Assistant

The most common errors [in college papers] are misuse of words and the perceived need to use convoluted constructions instead of simple declarative sentences. I think that's because students hide what they don't know in a torrent of words, in the hope that I won't notice.

—Samuel Diamond, Professor of Political
Science, University of Pennsylvania

Many students like to use polysyllabic words that impart no meaning. Students seem to feel that using larger words will impress the reader, but the intelligent reader will see through this effort. Students often like to use flowery phrases, purple prose, and inappropriate adjectives. I have seen essays that communicated so ineffectively that I had no idea what the students were trying to say.

—Michael F. Lane, Professor of Journalism
and Public Information, Emerson University

Another problem that I frequently see is that of the "reach exceeding the grasp." College students often want to sound sophisticated, and will try to use fancy words or imitate what they imagine "academic" writing to be, but the results are often stilted or odd.

—John Bendix, Professor of Women's
Studies, University of Pennsylvania

One thing professors dislike in a paper is "loaded language." The more precise and to the point one is when writing a paper, the better the grade. There is no need to be using vocabulary you don't really know, and there is no need to have five nicely worded sentences about one small thought; getting to the point is what makes professors happy.

—Chad Stansberry, Colorado University,
communications major

Students want to sound profound. The result is that they write with too much intensity and verbosity.

—Joseph Angotti, Professor at Northwestern
University

While you should examine each word with special scrutiny, these ideas should not be interpreted as a moratorium on all words that your five-year-old brother doesn't understand. He learned what a bulldozer was just last week. Big words can be appropriate, insightful, and helpful to the flow of your paper.

> A writer lives in awe of words, for they can be cruel or kind, and they can change their meanings right in front of you. They pick up flavors and odors like butter in a refrigerator.
>
> —John Steinbeck

I frequently remind students to make regular use of a good dictionary and a thesaurus. Obvious advice, to be sure, but advice that many students neglect to put into practice. It's through these tools of the writer's trade that a student discovers the best words for the sentences he or she is writing and revising—the sentences that he or she is trying to get just right. When we write, often a word will come to mind that sounds good, or at least good enough, but that turns out, when we check the dictionary, not to be the word that we really want for this or that particular context. Make the effort to find out for certain what your words mean—that's the job that the dictionary will help you to perform. And become acquainted with the family of words within which a specific word belongs—here, the thesaurus will come to your aid. The words for an entry in a thesaurus do not all mean the same thing. They are related to one another, but each one has its own implication of meaning. Keep your thesaurus nearby, next to the dictionary.

> —William E. Cain, Mary Jewett Gaiser
> Professor of English, Wellesley
> University

I was taught that everything is in the delivery. The choice of a word is a moment of truth for both the writer and the reader. Clarify and specify. The choice of a word is least of all about varying similar words or selecting a thesaurus search on the computer. Better to use a dictionary and to think about what a word means.

> —Jonathan Imber, Professor of Ethics,
> Wellesley College

wegotism: excessive use of the word *we*

Avoid Slang and Clichés

A cliché is an analogy characterized by its overuse. It may be true ("Fat as a pig"), no longer true ("work like a dog") or inscrutable ("right as rain"), but it has been overused to the point that its sole function is to mark its user as a lazy thinker.

Avoid clichés like the plague. Why? You need to convince your reader that you have something new and insightful to say. If your paper rests on endless clichés or common metaphors, the reader will subconsciously begin to doubt your originality and creativity.

Since the English language boasts over one million words, you have little excuse to use the crutches of clichés. Here are some clichés that might inadvertently creep into your writing.

Cliché Hit List

read something into it	eat your heart out
he's his own worst enemy	fact of the matter
come full circle	a slap in the face
from time immemorial	live dangerously
get the lead out	the road to recovery
it goes without saying	try as you may
the road of life	take a raincheck
sharp as a pin	let sleeping dogs lie
fair-weather friend	time will tell
hard nose	with all due respect
face as white as a sheet	it will be hard to try and fill his shoes

Sports jargon seems to creep in [to students' papers] almost daily. For example, "take it to another level" (e.g., "Woodrow Wilson really took it to another level when he declared war on Germany"), and "bring it to the table" ("As a political [candidate], Bryan brought many liabilities to the table").

—Andrew Rotter, Professor of History, Colgate University

Don't become lazy in your word choice. Thesauruses and creativity will equip you with the tools to sidestep those common phrases that lessen your credibility as an inventive writer.

Be Specific

Just as a viable thesis demands specific evidence to support it, so also does each sentence demand specific words for clarity. Tell your reader as much as possible by picking the most specific word for the situation. Goethe illustrated this idea when he remarked, "The poet should seize the particular; and he should, if there be anything in it, thus represent the universal."

> It ⇨ **Beverage** ⇨ **Juice** ⇨ **Snapple** ⇨ **Snapple's Diet Raspberry Tea**

If you're writing about "the car," explain that it's a "sleek Lamborghini." Instead of a "player on the team," refer to him as "the Reds' shortstop." Instead of "the evening," explain that it was "7:00 P.M."

In specificity there lies a risk of wordiness and complexity. Temper specifics, therefore, with more general words. Once you've established that the murderer was "the Reds' shortstop," you may use *him* in the next sentence. If you've already used *it* to describe the "sleek Lamborghini," feel free to use the generic *sports car*.

> Leo Tolstoy, the author of *War and Peace,* said, "I don't tell; I don't explain. I show; I let my characters talk for me." Writing that "shows" uses language that is specific, definite and concrete. It is the kind of language that helps the reader see a picture. Consider the following "show" and "tell" versions of the same sentences:
>
> *Tell* the local playground is in disrepair.
>
> *Show* At the local playground, weeds poke through cracked concrete and climb over collapsed, rusted swing sets.
>
> *Tell* Suddenly I awoke, frightened.
>
> *Show* Suddenly I awoke in a drenching sweat, my heart racing.

ogdoad: a group of eight

Tell	The trees by the water are filled with birds frantically look-ing for insects.
Show	The budding maples and birches overhanging the brook are alive with yellow-rumped warblers darting from twig to twig in a search for early insects.

—James W. Tankard, Professor of
Journalism, University of Texas—Austin

Use the Most Descriptive Words Available

Meaningless words often surface in academic writing. Passages may be long but entirely devoid of meaning. One source of meaningless words are those for which there are multiple definitions and interpretations.

Examples:
values, democracy, freedom, quality, justice, area, progressive, equality, science, idea, entity, attitude

While it may be difficult to eliminate the word *freedom* when discussing Alexis de Tocqueville's *Democracy in America,* you can create meaning to these words by defining them or by using adjectives that are descriptive and definite.

When using adjectives, avoid words that do not offer thorough description. Words like *small* and *little* can be replaced by more specific words like *scant* or *infinitesimal*. This more convincingly portrays your ideas to your reader.

If you're describing the type of day on which an event occurred, don't say "it was a nice day." What does "nice" mean in this context? Was the weather agreeable? Had events worked out so that conflict had been avoided? Indicate what you mean by replacing such a sentence with something like, "it was a beautiful day, thanks to the warm weather and sunshine."

Best-selling children's book author Jack Prelutsky, while writing *New Kid on the Block*, decided to replace *huge* with a more descriptive word. After perusing the thesaurus, he created a more descriptive poem:

> Seismosaurus was enormous.
> Seismosaurus was tremendous.
> Seismosaurus was prodigious.
> Seismosaurus was stupendous.
> Seismosaurus was titanic.
> Seismosaurus was colossal.
> Seismosaurus now is nothing,
> But a monumental fossil.

Avoid Boring, Ambiguous, and Overused Words

For the same reasons that clichés and general words should be avoided, you should try to replace boring, ambiguous, and overused words with more creative vocabulary. Below is a sampling of words that should rarely emerge in academic writing.

a little bit, a lot, actually, area, as far as . . . concerned, aspect, at least, awesome, big, boring, certainly, incidentally, interesting, involved with, just kind of, little, lots, nice, obviously, of course, particularly, phrase, predicament, pretty, problem, somehow, something like, somewhat, sort of, specially, stuff, surely, thing, too, totally, tremendously

Don't Overuse the Verb *to Be*

To be or not to be? When it comes to good writing, "not to be" will most likely be your answer. The verb "to be" can be overused. Its construction is weak; writing that eliminates the "to be" verbs undergoes remarkable change. Many career counselors advise that résumés use "power verbs." Using power verbs makes your resume more specific and forceful. Just as employers are more impressed with the specific and forceful résumé, so also will professors be impressed with writing that applies stronger verbs.

> **anthropolyglot:** a parrot or any other animal that can talk like a human

The best piece of writing advice I ever received drastically changed my entire writing style. One of my teachers in high school recommended that I go through my paper and eliminate every "to be" verb. Perhaps "recommended" is not the appropriate word choice: She said that she would deduct a point for every "to be" verb that I couldn't remove. I, the ever-zealous student, went through my paper and found that almost every sentence had some form of a "to be" verb. Removing the "to be" verb forced me to seek stronger verbs. This replacement required more than just a simple substitution of words: Often, I had to restructure the entire sentence to accommodate the more forceful verb. As I made these changes, however, I noticed that my writing flowed more smoothly and pleasantly. Today I remember this advice each time I am tempted to use a "to be" verb in my writing. Sure, the "to be" verb is not always inappropriate and weak; removing an "is" or "was" may result in an unnecessarily convoluted sentence. I've found, though, that the more forceful verbs foster simpler, more concise writing.

—Anonymous student, Yale University

Decent
Lemonade stands are great ways to earn a couple of extra quarters.

Better
Lemonade stands provide an excellent opportunity to earn a couple extra quarters.

GRAMMAR

In teaching writing, my greatest challenge lies in encouraging my students to play. They are generally well prepared and are very achievement oriented, but in some ways this hampers them. So concerned are they with "getting it right" that they inhibit themselves from engaging in the very activities which would improve their writing: experimenting with language, and pursuing their curiosity with words. I can teach students how to "do it right," but it is much harder to teach them the one thing that will guarantee their improvement—a love of writing

—Patrick Rael, Assistant Professor of
History, Bowdoin College

TOP-TEN METHODS OF PROCRASTINATION

According to student responses.

1. Play Freecell on the computer.
2. Learn to play the ukelele.
3. Check your e-mail/voice mail. Check again.
4. Download MP3s of songs you don't really like.
5. Write e-mails to friends at other colleges telling them about how busy you are.
6. Call the *Who Wants to Be a Millionaire* hotline. Repeatedly.
7. Surf the Internet.
8. Read junk mail, including credit card applications and those crappy college magazines they keep sending you for no apparent reason.
9. John Madden 2000/NHL 2000 (tie).
10. Talk to the little paper clip man who pops up on Microsoft Word whenever you push F1.

Ego sum rex Romanus, et supra grammaticam. [I am the Roman king and am above grammar.]

—Sigismund, Holy Roman Emperor

We're willing to put money down that you are not the Roman emperor, and so teacher probably will not buy the "I am above grammar" declaration. If, however, you actually *are* the Holy Roman Emperor, we humbly plead Your forgiveness and ask that we be spared from the lions.

It's advisable, therefore, that you give some attention to those seemingly nitpicky grammar rules. Don't excuse this attention to grammar as "kindergarten stuff." Professors often complain that the "all I need to know I learned in kindergarten" rule doesn't seem relevant anymore because 1) students never learned grammar in kindergarten (or any other grade, for that matter), or 2) students have forgotten the grammar they did learn in kindergarten.

> **twangdillo:** a sound made by playing a ukulele

> Every year, I encounter the occasional student in a literature course who argues that this or that essay he or she wrote should have received a better grade because the ideas are evident even though the student acknowledges that the essay is stylistically and grammatically flawed. Some students erroneously believe that a poorly expressed argument or idea is somehow as weighty and convincing and clear as a well-expressed argument or idea. This is simply not the case, but if students have been encouraged to believe that they can and should freely express themselves in writing with little regard to grammar and style, then it becomes quite difficult to get such students to take grammatical and stylistic issues seriously. Such students might tend to believe that they have all these exciting and profound ideas to explore and express, and learning grammatical rules and structures will simply cause them to expend good energy and effort on drudgery when they could be fruitfully expressing themselves.
>
> —Glyne A. Griffith, Professor of Literature, Bucknell University

Unfortunately (or fortunately, depending on how intensely you despise grammar), we cannot discuss every grammar point you learned or should have learned in kindergarten through your senior year of high school. Instead, this section will *generally* cover the *general* areas where students *generally* commit their grammar errors. Surveys of professors have revealed that these are their top complaints, so it might be helpful to consider some of the information below.

FIFTEEN DEADLY GRAMMAR SINS AND HOW YOU MAY BE SAVED

1. Thou Shalt Not End a Sentence in a Preposition

Ending a sentence or phrase with a preposition is like fingernails scraping a chalkboard for traditionalist writers (a category that your professors might fall under...whoops). While ending a sentence with a preposition is an accepted practice in speech, it's inappropriate in academic writing.

You can fix this problem by changing the order of the words.

Incorrect
This is the gigantic cup that you put Slurpees into.

Correct
This is the gigantic cup into which you put Slurpees.

Incorrect
"Why water fountains should be replaced with Slurpee machines" is the topic I want to write about.

Correct
"Why water fountains should be replaced with Slurpee machines" is the topic about which I want to write.

Sometimes, however, this sentence construction sounds stuffy. Let's face it: Writing, "that's the team on which I would like to play" is confusing—at least that's what Winston Churchill thinks. When reprimanded for ending a sentence with a preposition (the English are apparently really sensitive about good grammar), he replied: "This is the sort of thing up with which I will not put." For clarity's sake, it might be better to rewrite the sentence completely.

Incorrect
Where's the Slurpee sale going on?

Correct
Where is the Slurpee sale?

Incorrect
When's the Slurpee sale going on?

Correct
On what date is the Slurpee sale?

snurp: to shrivel

Grammar Dustup

A friendly, ruggedly good-looking Yale student was waiting in line to get a ticket to the Yale-Harvard football game, and behind him was a typically pretentious Harvard snob. Because he felt sorry for the poor guy who would have to watch his wimpy team go down in yet another defeat, the Yale student struck up a conversation.

"So, where are you from?" the Yale student politely asked.

Ignoring the question and raising his nose even further into the air, the Harvard student refused to answer. Instead, he replied pompously, "At Harvard, we do not end our sentences in prepositions."

Undaunted by the rudeness that Yalies have come to expect from their inferior counterparts, the Yalie tried again: "Excuse me," he said, "Where are you from, jerk?"

2. Thou Shalt Not Let Thy Modifiers Confuse Thy Reader

Modifiers are clauses, phrases, or individual words that influence the meaning of other words. Where these modifiers are positioned greatly affects the meaning of a sentence. Often misplaced modifiers inadvertently seep into writing. What makes misplaced modifiers so dangerous is that they expertly disguise themselves from the author but they loudly scream to the reader. To avoid such confusion, place the modifiers close by the words they modify; this placement should eliminate any confusion about what *exactly* is being modified.

Confusing Dependent Clauses

Dependent or subordinate clauses should be constructed so that the reader doesn't have to struggle to solve a mystery. Reading the paper aloud, one of the editing strategies suggested in the previous chapter, will help you catch logic problems such as the ones in the following examples.

> Forget grammar and think potatoes.
>
> —Gertrude Stein

Incorrect

After Jenny spent $479 on banjo strings, Jenny's parents suspended the credit card that she had for two weeks. (Did she have the credit card for two weeks, or did her parents suspend her spending privileges for two weeks?)

Correct

After Jenny spent $479 on banjo strings, Jenny's parents took away their credit card for two weeks.

Incorrect

The girl was given a makeover by a crew of noted makeup artists that was long overdue. (This says that the crew was long overdue.)

Correct

The girl was given a makeover that was long overdue by a crew noted makeup artists.

Incorrect

The stranded sailors sent bottles to twenty-seven merchants that had a message that asked for help. (This says that the merchants had a message that asked from help)

Correct

The stranded sailors sent bottles that contained a message that asked for help to twenty-seven merchants.

Misplaced Prepositional Phrases

Misplaced prepositional phrases are a source of confusion, and sometimes, unintentional humor.

Incorrect

The school reopened after summer vacation on August 29. (Was the vacation on August 29, or did the school reopen on August 29?)

Correct

After summer vacation, school opened on August 29.

zygal: anything shaped like the letter "h"

Also Correct
On August 29, school reopened after summer vacation.

Incorrect
The fire was started by two pyromaniacal kids in a trashcan. (That must have been a big trashcan to hold two children!)

Correct
The fire was started in a trashcan by two pyromaniacal kids.

Incorrect
The subject of this meeting is the risk of food poisoning in Bermuda. (Do Bermuda and food poisoning have some sort of connection?)

Correct
The subject of this meeting in Bermuda is the risk of food poisoning.

The Dreaded Dangling Participle

Practically all verbs in English can be turned into adjectives by adding either -*ed* or -*ing* to the basic form of the verb. The adjectival forms are called participles. Participles usually appear in participial phrases that modify another word in the sentence. The position of a participial phrase in a sentence is important. The phrase should be placed so that it clearly connects to the word it modifies. Don't let your participles dangle!

Incorrect
Rolling around in my car's ash tray, I found the marble I'd lost. (This says "I" was rolling around.)

More Correct
I found the lost marble rolling around in my car's ash tray. (Note that this sentence is also unclear: Did you find the marble while rolling around?)

Incorrect
We saw a one-eyed, one-horned, flying purple people eater driving down the road. (This says the a one-eyed, one-horned, flying purple people eater was driving.)

Correct
Driving down the road, we saw a one-eyed, one-horned, flying purple people eater.

Errant Adverbs

The biggest culprit for misplaced modifying words are adverbs, those *-ly* words: *only, hardly, nearly, scarcely, briefly, quickly, especially, claustrophobically, friendly, very*. And some others too: *not, even, almost*.

Incorrect
I only have been skipping for a short distance. (This could mean I, alone, have been skipping for a short distance.)

Correct
I have been skipping for only a short distance.

Double Take

Watch out for constructions in which a modifier is placed between two objects, either of which it might modify.

Prepositional Phrases

Incorrect
We concurred on the next day to storm the guys' room with a massive artillery of water balloons and squirt guns. (This sentence could mean either "We concurred to storm the guys' room with a massive artillery of water balloons and squirt guns on the next day" or "On the next day we concurred to storm the guys' room with a massive artillery of water balloons and squirt guns.")

Correct
We agreed that on the next day we would storm the guys' room with a massive artillery of water balloons and squirt guns.

OR: On the next day we concurred that we would invade their room with a massive artillery of water balloons and squirt guns.

mamamouchi: a bogus name or title

Incorrect
Amelia said in the morning she would shave her head.

Correct
In the morning, Amelia said she would shave her head.

OR: Amelia said that in the morning she would shave her head.

Dependent (Subordinate) Clauses

Incorrect
Miss America promised when she was on her way to Atlantic City to save the world.

Correct
When she was on her way to Atlantic City, Miss America promised to save the world.

OR: Miss America promised to save the world when she was on her way to Atlantic City.

Adverbs

Incorrect
The girl who slaved over her homework reluctantly accepted a full scholarship.

Correct
The girl who reluctantly slaved over her homework accepted a full scholarship.

OR: The girl who slaved over her homework accepted a full scholarship reluctantly.

Incorrect
The scarecrow only lacked a brain.

Correct
The scarecrow lacked only a brain.

Different Meanings

Often a modifier is not obviously out-of-place to readers; they simply misunderstand what you have written.

Incorrect
Trash has been converted into a protein-rich feline food with a high paper content. (The food has the high paper content?)

Correct
Trash with a high paper content has been converted into a protein-rich feline food.

Incorrect
We almost won all the games. (So, was each game really close?)

Correct
We won almost all of the games.

Incorrect
You only can prevent forest fires. (The only thing you can do, besides brushing your teeth, is prevent forest fires.)

Correct
Only you can prevent forest fires. (You're the only one, besides Smoky, who can prevent forest fires.)

3. Thou Shalt Not Split Thine Infinitives

Since they creep into oral speech so regularly, split infinitives are often ignored or disregarded in writing. Split infinitives, however, can obscure your meaning. To maintain clarity, watch where you put your modifying adverbs or adjectives and be sure that the infinitive is not interrupted.

pandiculation: stretching or yawning

Incorrect
She helped **to** quickly **cook** the macaroni and cheese.

Correct
She helped to cook the macaroni and cheese quickly.

OR: She quickly helped to cook the macaroni and cheese.

Incorrect
To furiously **slam** the brakes when a car is behind you can contribute to an accident.

Correct
To slam the brakes furiously when a car is behind you can contribute to an accident.

4. Thou Shalt Not Shift Verb Tenses

My pet peeve is when students go from past to present back to past tense again, often in the same paragraph.

—Lynn Marie Hoffman, Professor of
Education, Bucknell University

Nothing confuses your professor more than when you change your verb tenses. Parallel verb tenses can be a challenge, particularly when you're arguing that something should have been, might have been, will be, or was projected to be. The following tips should provide you with the tools to maintain verb continuity.

Stick with One Tense

Select a single tense and use it as your primary point of reference. Generally, this tense will be either present or past tense.

Use the present tense to refer to an activity that is going on right now.

Example
Bill Fitch **is** a masochistic circus performer known as the Human Pincushion.

Example
The NAAV, the North American Association of Ventriloquists, **is** a prosperous organization with 492 members.

Use the past tense for something that is over.

Example
Bertha Dlugi **invented** a diaper for a parakeet.

Example
Stevelandjudkins Morris **was** Stevie Wonder's original name.

Once the base tense is selected, be consistent. Committing to a tense doesn't mean that you've signed the line, promising to use past tense until death do you part. Just make sure that you use this tense as a base, changing it to convey the changes in time that your subject requires.

Example
When the Gilligan's Island Fan Club was founded in 1975, about 403,495 members were enrolled, and today, the number is still high.

Example
My morning routine is pretty, well, routine: I get up, brush my teeth, and wash my face. But on that fateful morning, I wasn't able to get up, brush my teeth, or wash my face.

Some Conventions to Note

Tenses do not always follow "actual time"; instead, there are conventions that dictate which tense is appropriate. Describing these conventions can become kind of sticky and convoluted. Don't worry: We'll give you those sticky and convoluted explanations. In addition, however, there are some examples that will better explain how certain tenses should be applied in certain situations.

> **penelopize:** to take apart and put back together to kill time

A dependent clause that is the object of a verb in the past tense is usually put in the past tense even though it refers to an existing state of affairs:

Example
You didn't tell me **you were busy!** (You **are** still busy…that is, until the five hundred pages of reading, three paper assignments, and four hundred commitments disappear, you will be busy.)

Example
What did you say your name was? (Your name still is Muriel Atanasoff.)

When the dependent clause describes a timeless state of affairs, the present tense may be used:

Example
The professor said that I am her favorite, brightest, and most modest pupil.

Example
They asked if I am available to take a "business trip" to Cancun next week.

When direct discourse is changed to indirect discourse (i.e., put into a dependent clause), its verb is usually shifted from present to past.

Direct
I am practicing.

Indirect
She said she was practicing.

Direct
I am becoming a toilet bowl salesman.

Indirect
He said he was becoming a toilet bowl salesman.

Dependent Clauses

Usually, when the tense of the independent clause is either present or past, the dependent clause follows in the same tense pattern:

Example
He wants to call the *Who Wants to Be a Millionaire?* hotline because he hopes to meet the dapper Regis Philbin.

Example
He wanted to call the *Who Wants to Be a Millionaire?* hotline because he hoped to meet the dapper Regis Philbin.

When the independent clause is in the future, repeating the future in the dependent clause is awkward, so shift to the present tense:

Example
He will get the $500 question wrong because he needs to use his lifelines on the first three questions.

Similarly, when the main verb is in either the present perfect or the future perfect tense, use the present tense:

Example
He has written the periodic table on his palm because he expects Regis to ask some chemistry questions.

Example
He will have written the periodic table on his palm because he expects Regis to ask some chemistry questions.

If the main verb is past perfect, the dependent verb is past tense.

Example
He had called his mother for help because he forgot the name of the main characters on *Happy Days*.

trichotillomania: an abnormal urge to pull out one's own hair

Example

He had called his mother for help because he had forgotten the name of the main characters on *Happy Days*.

When the independent and dependent clauses express the result of a hypothetical or nonfactual condition, the result is in the future or the conditional future perfect tense:

Example

If you insult Regis, you will get the tar beaten out of you.

Example

If you had insulted Regis, you would have gotten the tar beaten out of you.

5.Thou Shalt Not Let Your Subject and Verb Disagree

Here's how to check for trouble.

Example

The wombats, disturbed from their natural habitat by continual construction of retirement homes, were forced to take up residence behind the Slurpee machine in the 7-11.

- Pick out the subject of the sentence *(wombats)*.
- Find the main verb *(were forced)* and make sure it agrees in number.

Yes, this sentence is fine. Poor wombats.

Subject-verb agreement problems are most common when the subject and the verb are separated by a long prepositional phrase. Remember that prepositional phrases can always be removed from a sentence without changing its meaning.

6. Thou Shalt Not Let Your Pronouns Disagree

Example

This is an illustration of why the government needs to set money aside for wombat preservation and for posting warning notices on Slurpee machines.

- Find any and all pronouns in the sentence. In the sentence above it's *this*. Make sure to check for *this, they, their, them, it*.
- Look for the noun in the sentence that the pronoun is referring to. When you find the noun, check to be sure the pronoun agrees in number and person.
- Each of your sentences needs to have self-contained pronouns (the noun the pronoun is referring to must be in the same sentence). The example sentence is not correct, because "this" does not replace a noun from the sentence. Change the sentence to "This *situation* is an illustration" to correct the error.

7. Thou Shalt Not Forget to Be Parallel

Parallelism refers to the balance of two or more elements in a sentence. Elements in a sentence are parallel when one construction (or one part of speech) matches another: a phrase and a phrase, a clause and a clause, a verb and a verb, a noun and a noun, a gerund and a gerund, and so forth.

Just as a transition word helps the paper flow, so also does parallel structure aid in its smooth delivery.

Correctly deployed parallel structure can be a dramatic stylistic tool. Parallel structure makes a statement more emphatic, more noteworthy, and more eloquent. It requires creativity, demands attention to grammar, and necessitates a whole bunch of commas.

Parallel sentences tend to be catchy or eloquent, making them easy to recall. Campaign speech writers aim at pithy, parallel slogans, and statements that the politician's listener can easily remember.

tegestologist: a collector of cardboard beer coasters

In a speech to college students, one of Senator McCain's phrases stuck out more than any others: "Whether Democrat or Republican, vegetarian or Libertarian, students your age need to be involved in the political process."

Because of the parallel structure that he employed, the statement is easy to remember verbatim. See if you recognize any of these instances of parallel structure:

"Neither a borrower nor a lender be." (Shakespeare)

"Injustice anywhere is a threat to justice everywhere" (Martin Luther King Jr.)

"We shall fight on the beaches. We shall fight on the landing grounds. We shall fight in the fields and in the streets. We shall fight in the hills. We shall never surrender." (Winston Churchill)

"Ask not what your country can do for you, but what you can do for your country." (John F. Kennedy/Pierre Salinger)

"I came, I saw, I conquered." (Julius Caesar, as translated from Latin)

Give yourself two points for each quote you know by heart, an additional one point if you an identify the parallel structure, and six points if you can touch your nose with your tongue.

Sophisticated writing will undoubtedly incorporate parallelism into its paragraphs, but improper use of parallel structure will only make your paper appear elementary. You should consider the following when writing a sentence or paragraph with parallelism:

Noun + Noun + Noun

Not Parallel

For Christmas, Forrest Gump asked Santa for a pair of running shoes, a box of chocolate, and to get some shrimp recipes.

Parallel

For Christmas, Forrest Gump asked Santa for a pair of running shoes, a box of chocolate, and a shrimp recipe.

Verb + Verb

The verbs must be in the same tense and the same number (plural, singular).

Not Parallel

Forrest Gump beats Lieutenant Dan in races because the Lieutenant had no legs.

Parallel

Forrest Gump beats Lieutenant Dan in races because the Lieutenant has no legs.

Adjective + Adjective

Not Parallel

Bubba Gump Shrimp Company owns the lovely boat named after Jenny, who is best described as "vivacious."

Parallel

Bubba Gump Shrimp Company owns the lovely boat that is named after the vivacious Jenny.

Participle + Participle

Not Parallel

Owning thousands of shares of Apple stock and to win a game show hosted by Regis Philbin are both signs that you might be a millionaire.

Parallel

Owning thousands of shares of Apple stock and winning a game show hosted by Regis Philbin are both signs that you might be a millionaire.

caltrop: a four-pointed device used to impede pursuit

Word to the Wise

Microsoft Word's grammar check can be a useful tool to give your paper a decent once-over, but it can't replace doing your own proofreading.

- On the toolbar, click "Tools" and select "Options." Click on "Spelling & Grammar" and select the "Settings" button under grammar. Here you have the option of expanding Word's grammar checking capabilities to look for commas in a series, punctuation in quotation marks, clichés, wordiness, and all kinds of other exciting proofreading options. To see how your writing stands up, try selecting everything and let the computer go to town.

- Word also includes some "helpful" features Microsoft calls AutoFormat and AutoCorrect. AutoFormat is responsible for automatically inserting a "2" every time you type the number "1" regardless of whether you want it or not. If you're making a list of items, it may serve you well, but otherwise it's a horrendous pain. AutoFormat can be disabled by going to the "Tools" menu, clicking "AutoCorrect," and selecting the "AutoFormat As You Type" tab. Improve your quality of life by getting rid of everything that irritates you, or turn off the automatic formatting altogether by clearing all options. If you want to have the computer reformat after you're done typing, you can still do this by selecting "AutoFormat" from the "Format" menu.

Infinitive + Infinitive

Not Parallel
Getting a box of chocolates is easy, but to know what is inside is quite difficult.

Parallel
To get a box of chocolates is easy, but to know what is inside is quite difficult.

Phrase + Phrase

Not Parallel

With braces on his legs and a head filled with nothing, Forrest was an ideal target for bullies.

Parallel

With braces on his legs and nothing in his head, Forrest was an ideal target for bullies.

8. Thou Shalt Not Bore Thy Reader with Unvaried Sentence Structure

Another way to ensure a coherent and flowing paper is to diversify sentence structure. Since you're probably not up for a full-fledged discourse on the elements of sentence structure, we'll briefly summarize. Sentences generally fall into one of the following types: simple sentences, compound sentences, complex sentences, and compound-complex sentences.

Simple sentences are the most basic structure.

> See Spot run.

> Old MacDonald had a farm.

Compound sentences join two or more simple sentences.

> Old MacDonald had a farm, and you can see Spot run on his premises.

Complex sentences add a dependent clause to a simple sentence (i.e., an independent clause).

> Although Old MacDonald had a farm, the farmer could not see Spot run because he was blind.

zinzolin: a violet color

Build Your Reader's Interest

Many years ago, when I was just beginning high school, I believed that good writing meant extremely complex, wordy sentence structures. The more difficult a paragraph was to plod through, the more thoughtful and academic it must have been. I packed my writing with passives, run-on sentences, and extremely convoluted structures to avoid any possibility of an overly colloquial or simplistic tone . . . When writing papers, you should continually be asking yourself if you can make your writing any clearer. Using overly complicated structures to affect a formal or detached tone simply makes your paper more dull and plodding. While a lively paper certainly varies sentence structure from time to time, it should not be so convoluted as to bury the central argument in weighty but unnecessary rhetoric. Ultimately your readers should find your writing clear and direct.

—Sharon Stanley, Dartmouth College Writing
Assistant

One of the most common problems I find in undergraduate papers is boring, repetitive prose—a long series of sentences, often short sentences, beginning with the subject. Students commit this kind of error because they have been taught all kinds of bad rules about writing in high school: Don't begin sentences with *and* or *but,* for instance. Because these rules hamstring students, making it difficult for them to write cohesive arguments, I encourage them to use the full structural resources of the language. They can begin sentences, I remind them, not only with the subject but in many other ways as well: with a subordinate clause, with a coordinate conjunction, with an adverb, with a preposition, with an infinitive, with a participial phrase, with the object, with a noun clause, with a question, and occasionally with a fragment. Once students understand that their prose has much more energy when they vary the structure and length of their sentences, they often feel empowered and write much more interesting prose.

—J. Dennis Huston, Professor of English,
Rice University

Compound-complex sentences are the most elaborate. They combine two or more independent clauses and one or more dependent clauses.

> Old MacDonald had a farm, but because he was blind, he could not see Spot run.

While other sentence structures exist, these are the most common. Mix and match them. Don't let all your sentences be simple, and don't let all of your sentences follow the compound-complex model. Let some sentences be long, meandering about, joining together shorter phrases and sentences into a long combination of phrases. Keep other sentences short.

Readers get bored when all sentences follow an identical pattern. Be nice to your readers: Provide diverse sentence structures that keep them awake.

Short sentences are often useful for making a dramatic point or emphasizing a particular piece of evidence; long sentences generally list a series of ideas, include a transition from one idea to another, or qualify an emphatic idea made in a short sentence. Don't become so consumed with sentence structure that it obfuscates your ideas, however.

A coherent paper emphasizes the especially important ideas for the reader. While writers use various sentence structures, words, and phrasings to emphasize, here are some general guidelines to consider.

- The end of a sentence is the most emphatic location. The next most emphatic spot is the beginning. Take a wild guess as to the least emphatic location in a sentence. That's correct: the middle. Therefore, make sure that you place the most considerable information in the beginning or ending of a sentence.
- If you're trying to make a smooth transition by introducing old evidence and merging in new ideas, put the old information before the new.
- Independent clauses tend to get more attention than dependent clauses.
- Anything that is placed out of order merits special attention from the reader.

arotophilist: a teddy bear collector

- Words that are differentiated by underlining, boldface, italics, or capital letters tend to receive special attention. Use font differentiation sparingly, however; it should be your words, and not your lettering, that create emphasis.
- Ideas that are contained in prepositional phrases rarely receive emphasis.

9. Thou Shalt Not Use the Subjective *I*

This is a point made by more than one professor, so don't just take it from *us*.

> Students too frequently use the first person and think that their opinion is of intrinsic interest and importance, and it is not. Students should avoid, in most instances, making remarks in the first person and from stating opinions as such. Too often their self-infatuation and their mothers' love promotes this. College education must do the opposite.
>
> —Barry Shain, Professor of Political Science, Colgate University

> The main problem I find is that students' essays are weakened by the propensity to insert their own, often personal opinions in colloquial language. While it's important for the student to understand why she agrees or disagrees personally with issues raised, the exercise is generally not about presenting these opinions. Steer clear of doing so unless explicitly invited to do so.
>
> —Linda Angst, Professor of Anthropology, Earlham College

10. Thou Shalt Not Abuse Commas

Separating Independent Clauses

Use commas between independent clauses. Compound sentences have two clauses. If the two clauses can stand by themselves, they're independent. If you join two independent clauses with a conjunction, use a comma.

Example
Slurpees are good, so **I drink them often**.

Clever Acronym?

You can remember what a conjunction is by this clever acronym: FANBOYS. If you contest the "cleverness" of this acronym, ignore this sidebar and go to the next sentence. If you're interested, however, read on:

F = *for*
A = *and*
N = *nor*
B = *but*
O = *or*
Y = *yet*
S = *so*

If you have two independent clauses and don't wish to join them with a conjunction (FANBOYS), you can use a semicolon instead of a comma.

Example
Slurpees are good; I drink them often.

If the two clauses cannot stand by themselves, don't use a comma.

Example
I enjoy Slurpees and drink them often.

Comma Splices

A comma splice occurs when you have what should be a compound sentence, but you neglect to include the conjunction joining the two complete sentences.

Incorrect
The wombats burst out of the 7-11, they ran amok through the streets.

Correct the comma splice by either adding the missing conjunction or by replacing the comma with an impressive-looking semicolon.

ullage: the unfilled space in a barrel or wine bottle

Correct
The wombats burst out of the 7-11, and they ran amok through the streets.

Or:

The wombats burst out of the 7-11; they ran amok through the streets.

It's also possible that you should split your run-on sentence into two, Hemingway style.

Correct
The wombats burst out of the 7-11. The creatures ran amok through the streets.

Commas and Dates

Incorrect
February, 2982

Correct
February 2982

Only use a comma if you need to separate a particular day from the year.

Correct
February 7, 2982

Appositions

An apposition is a construction in which a noun or noun phrase is placed with another as an explanatory equivalent.

Appositions are used to supplement information about a word or phrase. When you say, "I spent the day doing my favorite activity, trying to catch leprechauns," the appositives are "my favorite activity" and "trying to catch leprechauns." The second appositive specifies the first.

Surround the appositional phrase with commas.

Example
Regis Philbin, a dapper dresser with a million-dollar smile, is my idol.

Phrases within a Sentence
Setting off phrases with commas can change a sentence's meaning:

Example
7-11 owners who keep pet wombats are in violation of city ordinances.

Example
7-11 owners, who keep pet wombats, are in violation of city ordinances.

The second sentence implies that *all* 7-11 owners keep pet wombats and are in violation of city ordinances, while the first sentence says that not all 7-11 owners have wombats, but *those that* do are in violation.

If a phrase is set off by commas, it can be removed without changing the meaning of the sentence. These phrases basically contain "by the way" sorts of information. So in the previous example, the second sentence can be rewritten to say, "7-11 owners are in violation of city ordinances," which is obviously not the case. Commas should not have been used in this situation, so the first sentence is the correct one (unless all 7-11 owners actually do have pet wombats). Be sure to only set off nonessential phrases with commas or you'll change the meaning of the sentence.

Titles and Degrees
Commas should be used to separate titles and degrees from names.

Example
Homer Simpson, CEO of Beer-Drinking Couch Potatoes Anonymous (BDCPA).

umami: the fifth taste

Lists

While people debate whether a comma is essential before the last item of a list, your safest bet is to use it. Omitting the final comma can confuse a reader.

Example
I would like to thank the Academy, my parents, and God.

When you have a list that separates every object with *and, nor,* or *or,* there's no need to insert commas.

Example
Slurpees and Fat Boy ice cream sandwiches and Big Gulp sodas and greasy hotdogs are available at 7-11.

After Dependent Clauses

When you have an introductory phrase like this one, it is necessary to isolate it from the rest of the sentence by putting a comma after it. On occasion, however, short introductory clauses do not need a comma. Read the sentence aloud. Do you pause after the short clause? If you do, insert a comma.

Example
To properly prepare a wombat, you should use copious amounts of dillweed.

For Clarity

Commas may be replaced by semicolons if the replacement makes a sentence clear. When a sentence has long, descriptive lists, or when a sentence uses commas for various reasons (you might have a list with various dates), substituting a semicolon for a comma is acceptable.

Example
I will be in town on March 20, 2000; April 2, 2000; and August 17, 2000.

11. Thou Shalt Not Abuse Apostrophes

Possessive

The most basic form of a possessive in English is the "apostrophe s" construction.

> Susan's eye
> Justin's stupidity
> Marti's lack of creativity
> A penny's worth

Plural possessives can be trickier. When the plural ends in *s*, simply place the apostrophe after the word.

> The house of the Jetsons ⇨ The Jetsons' house
> Two hours' work

Beware of words that are already plural.

> **Women's**, not **womens'**; **People's**, not **peoples'**; **children's**, not **childrens'**

Possessive pronouns don't get apostrophes. Sorry.

> **Theirs**, not **their's**; **hers**, not **her's**; **whose**, not **who's**; **its**, not **it's**

Use "it's" only to mean "it is," not to show possession.

> **Example**
> Raquel discovered that **it's** not a good idea to pat a wombat on **its** head while **it's** eating **its** supper.

Drop apostrophes when you make abbreviations or acronyms plural.

> **Incorrect**
> I got a 1600 on my SAT's.

threap: to rebuke; to maintain persistently; to insist on; to urge, to press eagerly; to contradict

Correct (but not true)
I got a 1600 on my SATs.

If the apostrophe-less acronym is confusing, put an apostrophe in.

Incorrect
I got all As this semester.

Correct (but also not true)
I got all A's this semester.

Years

Use a flipped apostrophe if you eliminate the first two numbers of a year, but do not use an apostrophe before the *s*.

Incorrect
1980's, '80's

Correct
1980s, '80s

Quotes

Use individual apostrophes when there's a quote within a quote.

My roommate said, "Marti, if you don't stop saying 'cool,' I'll get my entire rugby team to beat you up."

12. Thou Shalt Not Ignore Capitalization Rules

Rule One

Capitalize the first word of a sentence.

Example
Anyone who doesn't know this rule is a moron.

Major Words of a Title

Example

My favorite book is *Curious George and the Mysterious Puzzle Piece.*

Proper Nouns, Names, Acronyms, Titles

Examples

Elvis Presley

HUD

Spain

Madame Defarge

Weird Ones

- *Renaissance* and *Romantic* should be capitalized when they refer to historical periods. If they refer to rebirth or widespread ability or romance, don't capitalize them.
- *Middle Ages* is capitalized, but *medieval* is not.
- *President* should be capitalized when you're referring to a specific person:

Example

President Clinton

But do not capitalize it when it's general:

Example

The president of the company

duende: literally a ghost, goblin, demon; inspiration, magnetism, ardor

13. Thou Shalt Never Use Run-On Sentences or Fragments

Most students simply don't know three pillars of grammar: what a comma splice is, the difference between a colon and semicolon, and the difference between *affect* and *effect*. What I like to do is to explain all three very quickly right at the beginning. To be frank, most students I have told this to are really appreciative of this quick, two-minute refresher. Most want to know this information, but are quite embarrassed by the fact that they have forgotten these rules.

—Michael Farrell, Colby College, tutor for
Colby College Farnham Writers' Center

Sentence variety makes a paper more entertaining to read. Your professors will not be entertained, however, if they're fuming over the run-on sentences that you're using. A run-on sentence occurs when two sentences run into one without proper punctuation.

Two sentences glued together with only a comma separating them produce a comma splice, a kind of run-on.

Example
I like coffee, I like tea.

It's a cute song, but this punctuation is not grammatically correct. Change it to "I like coffee; I like tea," and the problem is solved. Another solution is to add one of those conjunctions: "I like coffee, and I like tea."

Fragments are incomplete sentences. Often, fragments are segments of sentences that have been detached from the main clause.

Incorrect
Slurpees come in many flavors. Like cherry, Coke, blue raspberry, and piña colada.

Correct
Slurpees come in many flavors like cherry, Coke, blue raspberry, and piña colada.

Incorrect

Wombats are no good at football. Because of their lack of opposable thumbs.

Correct

Wombats are no good at football because they're afraid of getting tackled.

Incorrect

After I screamed at the 7-11 manager for the disrepair of the machine, he stomped off. *Leaving me alone and irate.*

Correct

After I screamed at the 7-11 manager for the disrepair of the machine, he stomped off, leaving me alone and irate.

Incorrect

I need to find another example. *Because the readers are probably getting sick of Slurpees. Or thirsty.*

Correct

I need to find another example because the readers are either getting sick of Slurpees or becoming thirsty.

14. Thou Shalt Never Use the Wrong Word

accept, except

"I *accept* the universe." (Margaret Fuller) (receive, approve, tolerate)

Everyone at the party was rowdy. I *except* Clyde from the inquiry because he was unconscious at the time. (excuse)

affect, effect

Writing papers has a strange *effect* on me. (result)

Poems *affect* me deeply. (move, influence)

The government wants to *effect* a policy of partial disclosure. (bring about)

> **fleer:** to make wry faces in contempt; to jeer

Af•fect (n.) (psychology) Pronounced with emphasis on the first syllable, this *affect* means, according to *Webster's Tenth Dictionary*, the conscious subjective aspect of an emotion considered apart from bodily changes. That is, a person's *affect* is how she comes across: depressed, detached, wired, and so on.

allude, elude
She alluded to Lillian Hellman in her paper on the McCarthy Era. (referred)
The suspect *eluded* her pursuers. (evaded, escaped from)

all right
(two words) *Alright* is not all right.

a lot
(two words)

ambiguous, ambivalent
The language Plato uses is *ambiguous* in discussing death. Sometimes death is paradise; at other times it feels like hell. (suggestive of opposite ideas or feelings)
Plato obviously feels *ambivalent* about death. (torn between opposites)

anecdote, antidote
If you tell an amusing or instructive story, you're telling an *anecdote*.
If you're bit by a snake and require medical attention, you'll need an *antidote*, after which you can tell an anecdote about being bit by a snake.

aptitude, attitude
Aptitude is inclination or talent.
Attitude is a mental position.

beside, besides
Beside usually means by.
Besides usually means other than or except.
If used as an adverb, *besides* means moreover.

cite, sight, site
A good research paper will *cite* more than one authority on a subject. Congress *cited* the bureaucrat for contempt. (issue citations or make references)
The campers *sighted* Bigfoot leaping from peak to peak. (spotted visually)
The house was *sited* over an underground river. (situated)

collaborate, corroborate
Try taking these apart. To *collaborate* means to work with: i.e., *co-labor*.
Corroborate means to support with authority, to strengthen. (*robur* means strength, as in "robust.")

complacence, complaisance, compliance
Complacence means self-satisfaction.
Complaisance means affability.
Compliance means conformity or a disposition to give in to others.

complement, compliment
Complement suggests completion.
Compliment suggests praise.
When Zeke had eaten his full *complement* of crayfish, the crowd paid him the compliment of singing, "For He's a Jolly Good Fellow."

comprehensive, comprehensible
She took a *comprehensive* exam in economics. (covering all subjects)
She found the exam questions *comprehensible*. (understandable)

compose, comprise, constitute
Comprise means includes, as the whole comprises its parts. (is made up of)
Compose means make up or fashion, as a painting is composed of lines, colors, and texture.
Constitute can also mean compose, but is more often used in the active voice to show how a part stands for a whole: "Greed constitutes his major motive."

fardingbag: the first stomach of a cow

contemptible, contemptuous
Hellman thought McCarthy's methods *contemptible*. (worthy of contempt)
Hellman was *contemptuous* of McCarthy. (felt contempt for)

continual, continuous
By *continual* practice, she learned two of Chopin's Etudes. (frequently repeated)
The fire alarm made a *continuous* snarling whine. (without interruption, ceaseless)

counsel, council
Yes, you can *counsel* (give advice to) a *council* (meeting or group).

critique, criticize
Professor Richard Cody writes occasional *critiques* of movies for the *Hampshire Gazette*. (noun, meaning critical review)
I asked her to *criticize* my latest poem. (offer critical remarks on)

data
Believe it or not, *data* is plural, the plural of *datum*.
So, don't say "the data tells us," but "the data tell us," unless, of course, they don't. (Similarly *criteria* is the plural of *criterion* and *media* is the plural of *medium*.)

dilemma
Dilemma, not *dilemna*.

discrete, discreet
The book was divided into *discrete* sections, each written by a different author. (separate)
She was *discreet* about her former relationships. (tactful, discerning)

disinterested, uninterested
The ideal judge is informed, wise, and *disinterested*. (above all special interests; impartial)
I am usually *uninterested* in television, except on weekends. (not interested)

ecology, environment
We are studying the *ecology* of the Malaysian jungle. (relationship between organisms and environment)
We are afraid that nuclear waste will destroy the *environment*. (surroundings)

enervate, energize
Enervate means to tire out.
Energize means to give energy to.
Opposites!

ensure, insure, assure
These overlap when used to mean "make certain a specific outcome." But *ensure* means generally guarantee; insure implies taking specific measures to do so, to indemnify against liability; and *assure* has the connotation of "give support or comfort."

fewer, less
fewer in number, *less* in amount, i.e.:
Fewer people than last year showed up to see if the amount of beans in the jar was *less* than they had guessed.

flout, flaunt
Some people like to *flout* the idea of joining fraternities; others like to *flaunt* the fact that they've joined.
flout = mock, make fun of
flaunt = show off

hopefully
Hopefully describes how something is done or how the subject feels: "*Hopefully* I shall turn in this paper" does not mean "I hope I get it in," but "I shall turn in this paper in a hopeful manner."

illicit, elicit
The lovers had an *illicit* rendezvous. (outside the law)
The idea of a party will elicit everybody's approval. (garner, draw forth)

imminent, eminent, immanent
Adrienne Rich is an *eminent* (famous) poet whose appearance on campus is *imminent* (about to happen). Feminism is *immanent* (indwelling, present) in her work.

liripoop: the tassel on a college graduation cap

imply, infer

The speaker *implies* that UFOs exist. (suggests)

The hearer *infers* that the speaker believes in UFOs. (gathers, concludes)

incredible, incredulous

I was *incredulous* (astonished, unbelieving) when I heard the *incredible* (not-to-be-believed) news.

lead, led, lead

The Pied Piper *leads* the children of Hamelin.

Once upon a time he *led* the rats into the river.

After walking six miles up a mountain, his feet felt like *lead*.

leave, let

"Please *leave* immediately," said Greta Garbo. (depart from)

I want to be *let* alone. (allowed to be)

lie, lay

If you *lie* down with dogs, you will get up with fleas. (present tense of *lie*)

I *lay* down with dogs and got up with fleas. (past tense of *lie*)

Lay your weary body down. (present tense of *lay*, which takes an object)

He *laid* himself down on the bed. (past tense of *lay*)

like, as

"Where did you get that quiz of a hat? It makes you look like an old witch."

—Jane Austen, *Northanger Abbey* (*like*
matches up nouns or noun phrases)

"As when a dab-chick waddles through the copse
On wings and feet, and swims and flies and hops."

—Alexander Pope, "The Dunciad" (*as* goes
with verbs)

literally, figuratively

Do NOT say "My cousin Billy Bob is *literally* a horse's butt," unless you are a horse and Billy Bob has gone to the knacker's.

You can say, however, that your cousin Billy Bob is *figuratively* a horse's whatever if he is acting like one.

loan, lend

Use lend when you mean "*lend* a hand."

Use *loan* for a noun, meaning money lent at interest.

When used in connection with material goods, **loan** is, contrary to what some purists will tell you, a legitimate verb, as in "My cousin Billy Bob loaned me his horse van to use over vacation."

lose, loose

Don't set the fox loose in the henhouse or else we'll lose our chickens.

mitigate, militate

Mitigate means to soften or mollify, as you *mitigate* a blow to the ego with soft words.

Militate means to engage in warfare.

Opposites!

oral, verbal

I have to give an *oral* report in history class. (spoken)

My *verbal* skills need improvement. (having to do with words, either written or spoken)

phenomenon, phenomena

One *phenomenon*, several *phenomena.*

populous, populace

Los Angeles has a teeming *populace.* (noun, short for population)

New York is also quite *populous.* (adjective, meaning "filled with people")

nonillion: the number one followed by thirty zeros

preceding, proceeding
Preceding means going before, prior, or former.
Proceeding means advancing or moving along a course.

pretense, pretext
He was fired for not being a team player, but this was only a *pretext* for his not getting along with the insiders. (cover-up, false reason)
Those fancy phrases are all *pretense*. (vain show)

principle, principal
My high school *principal* was a fuddy-duddy. (short for principal person)
The *principal* cause of Nixon's Watergate mess was his anxiety about reelection. (main, chief)
The *principal* drew $200 interest. (capital sum)
I support your *principle*, but I disagree with your methods. (aim, ideal)

societal, social
Societal means exclusively "of or pertaining to society."
Social has many more meanings, such as "sociable," involving allies or confederates, or relating to the members of society, as in "social practices."

than, then
"First I'll pray, *then* I'll sleep." —Shakespeare, *King Lear* (adverb of time)
I like pizza better *than* Big Macs. (comparative conjunction)

their, there, they're
Students don't always turn *their* papers in on time, claiming that since *there* are too many deadlines, *they're* often too busy.

unique
Unique means one-of-a-kind.
That Victorian piano stool–barber's chair–footlocker is certainly *unique*. RIGHT.
He is a rather *unique* person. WRONG: He can't be rather one-of-a-kind.

wary, weary
Wary means suspicious.
Weary means tired (see enervate).

Some professors are weary of reading *wary* when the writer means weary. Such practices make them *wary* of reading papers.

—courtesy of the Amherst Writing Center, used by permission

15. Thou Shalt Not Forget How to Indicate Whether Something's a Book, Poem, Magazine, Etcetera

ITALICS
long poems
works of art
long musical compositions
books
magazines
newspapers
pamphlets
movies
plays
radio and television series

QUOTES
short poems
short musical compositions or songs
short stories
book
chapters
magazine or newspaper articles
individual radio and television episodes

staupings: the hoof marks of cattle

SPELLING

Your memory of weekly spelling quizzes and those annoying spelling bees sends shivers up your spine. You excuse yourself as a poor speller. Your professor won't

> "Tpyo? What tpyo?"
>
> —Kea d'Albenas

accept either excuse on your paper, so it's best that you learn the rules of spelling right now. If spelling is seriously a problem, get someone else to read your paper or look up words that you know you frequently misspell.

> Beginning students often struggle with basic spelling problems. Some students don't use the spelling-check feature on their computers or may rely on spell check too greatly. Most students don't have a dictionary or thesaurus by their computer, which would solve many writing problems. As a writing coach, I find it difficult to help students with loftier communication challenges when we have to spend so much time on the most elemental parts of sentence structure and basic grammar.
>
> —Michael Lane, Professor of Journalism and Public Information, Emerson University

Ways to Eliminate Spelling Errors while Proofreading

1. Highlight words you think might be incorrect. Look them up in the dictionary.

2. Look at each word and ask yourself whether you know what its appropriate spelling is. It's a yes-no question. If your answer is "it looks right," highlight that sucker and look it up.

3. Notice what part of the word you've spelled wrong. Usually you mess up on just a couple letters. If you can target those letters in the future, you'll be one step closer to becoming the International Spelling Champ.

The wohmbats arr qute, fuzy annimals lat lik to eet Twinkys and other Hostess produkts.

The spelling check feature on your computer is an extremely valuable tool (see sidebar on Microsoft Word spelling and grammar check). However, don't count on your spell check to bail you out of any situation.

> I spent a week in a hermetically sealed dorm room researching and typing out a thirty-page term paper. My thesis was that Colonial-era Mexican food was an inherently mestizo cultural artifact (*mestizo* meaning "mixed race" or multiethnic). At 10:20 on the morning it was due at 10:30, after having been up for ninety some hours, I sped it through one final spell check (I had edited extensively) before printing it out, running to the history department, and handing the still-warm paper to my rather amused TA. He had good reason to be amused later. Unbeknownst to me, the computer changed every single appearance of the word *mestizo* to *Maoist*, its closest approximation. Suddenly Maoist villagers were running around colonial Mexico, Maoist communities, Maoist farmers, and such were springing up. It was all very traumatic.
>
> —David Laibstain, Brown University

Remember that your spell checker tells you only if you've spelled a word correctly, not if you've spelled the *right* word correctly.

Wombats fined there weigh in the dark buy using they're scents of smell.

The spell check doesn't pick up anything out of the ordinary in the previous sentence, but its appearance in your paper would probably hurt your quest for a diploma. The point is, even after running the spell check, you should still read through a draft by hand and look for errors.

mallemaroking: carousing of seamen in icebound ships

PRESENTATION

Once the text of your paper is done, you're through the hard part. All that remains is to get the thing into a presentable form for your professor, brush your teeth, and crawl into bed.

> Just as those final words were penned, the sun broke out in power, and gladdened all things.
>
> —William Wordsworth

We hope that you've been printing out drafts of your paper as you've been going along, so you know where to find a usable, working printer. Whether it's on the desk of a roommate or over in a computer cluster, just knowing that a printer is sitting there, waiting to spew out your final draft, should give you a warm, fuzzy feeling inside.

Most of us have had the unpleasant shock of last-minute printing problems at some point during our academic careers. Maybe the university computer technicians decided that three in the morning the day your paper's due would be the ideal time to do maintenance work on the network. Or perhaps the only printer in the place is out of paper.

The best solution to these problems? Don't wait until the absolute last minute to finish your paper. We know this isn't a particularly popular solution, but it's the only one hundred percent effective one, much like abstinence is the best prevention of sexually transmitted diseases.

Having your own personal supply of printer paper can alleviate some of your worries also. If you have the choice, always use standard, 8.5 x 11-inch white paper. The thicker stuff with the fancy watermarks can give your work a more distinguished look, but the only real advantage is that the more expensive paper doesn't allow the ink to smudge as easily.

When asked, most professors will tell you that they want papers written double-spaced with standard, 12-point font and 1-inch margins. As with most every step of the paper writing process, we recommend that you follow your professor's guidelines exactly. Also as with most every step of the paper writing process, we realize that "bending" these guidelines a little is quite often necessary.

Let's say you've just completed an ingenious analysis of the effects of Kraft macaroni and cheese on migrant subcultures of rural Louisiana. You're positive every sentence in this paper lends perfect cohesiveness and clarity to your argument, and you're sure that changing a single word would be the equivalent of touching up the Mona Lisa with a paint roller. We don't believe you for a second, incidentally, but let's go along with the scenario for now. So the only problem with your impressive treatise is that it's a full page over the maximum length proscribed by your professor. What to do, what to do? Or, just as likely you've written a Hemmingway-esque little number that presents a clear, succinct argument that just happens to be, well, a little too succinct. A page too succinct, actually. What to do? What to do, naturally, is to bend the rules a little bit. As a side note, you're probably going to hell for this one, you immoral bastard.

stillicide: the steady drip of a raindrop

BENDING THE RULES
(or, Cheating and Deceiving Instead of Deleting)

Fonts

Your paper's font is probably the area of presentation in which you have the least leeway. Times New Roman has become almost a universal standard font for papers in recent years, and other styles are immediately obvious and will raise your professor's suspicions that you're up to something.

Arial is bigger and will add length to your paper, but is obviously different, especially when compared to a paper written in Times. It lends a certain elementary school quality to your work that cannot be considered desirable.

```
Courier New should not be used under any circumstances.
```

Verdict: Using anything other than Times New Roman (with the possible exception of Palatino, which doesn't come with Microsoft Word) is blatantly obvious and will make your professor laugh. Don't try it unless your real goal in life is to flunk out of college.

Margins

The *MLA Handbook for Writers of Research Papers,* the standard reference guide for these sorts of things, makes 1-inch margins all around the rule. The average professor knows these measurements and requires them for papers.

What's really interesting here, however (and what most students and professors don't realize) is that Microsoft Word's default settings are for 1-inch top and bottom margins, but 1.25 inches on the left and right sides. Since most everyone assumes that the defaults on a word processor would be universal standards, the extra .25 inches on either side of your text can combine for a hefty half inch useful for squeezing or expanding your paper.

The difference between 1.25 and 1.00 inch side margins is very difficult to detect visually, but can provide a nice impact, especially on longer papers. The smaller, 1.00 margins will typically allow about a line and a half of text more per page than the larger, 1.25 inch margins. A line and a half may not seem like much now, but over the course of a ten page paper these lines can add up to a half-page difference in page length. Remember also that if you must make one margin bigger to help increase length, it should be the left one. Since you staple on the left side, a bigger margin won't be as obvious.

Line Spacing

Altering the spaces in between lines is an old favorite trick of students who can't write to length, but it's also one of the more obvious (although not as obvious as changing the font). The key here is to expand or compress by fractions of a line, but not by so much that it becomes farcical. Increasing or decreasing the line spacing by .25 (to make it 2.25 or 1.75) doesn't look too terrible, although comparison with another standard paper will give you away. Changing the line spacing by a subtle .1 or so can add or take away a few valuable lines, but not get you caught.

Kerning

The most overlooked weapon in the lazy paper writer's arsenal is also one of the most useful. Kerning refers to the size of the spaces between letters, something that most people don't even notice. As with other tricks, make sure not to over-do kerning. A l i t t l e   b i t   c a n   g o   a   l o n g   w a y .

To play with kerning in Microsoft Word, select "font" from under the "Format" menu. Hit the tab for character spacing and select "expanding" or "compressing" depending on whether you've written too much or too little. Optimum kerning amounts are probably about .3 either way, although the desperate may be able to get away with .5. Changing the spacing by .5 can have a drastic affect on your paper, increasing an eight-pager to a full nine pages.

boondocking: a good shot in the game of tiddledywinks

Remember, if your paper is either way too long or far too short, it probably means you did a lousy job organizing the structure or didn't take enough time revising. Your best bet is to go back and take a hard look at your paper, rather than trying to find the easy way out by playing with fonts and margins. It may save you time now, but it's only going to hurt you later when you get your grade.

TITLE PAGES

If your professor doesn't give you specific instructions as to whether or not he wants you to use a title page, make the call yourself based on your personal preference and space considerations. If your paper is already at the maximum page length, go ahead and make a title page, while if you have room to spare, put your title information on the first page of your paper.

If you're not using a title page, include your name, your professor or TA's name, the class, and the date single-spaced and left-justified. Skip a space and write your title, centered. You don't need to put your title in quotes or italics.

Example
Lamar Higgins
Prof. St. Claire
Social Justice and Cookery 411
Feb. 2, 2001

The Ecclesiastical Implications of Kraft Macaroni and Cheese

A long time ago in a galaxy far, far, away.... And the body of the paper will continue here.

If you decide a title page is necessary, put the same information on the page, but all centered. Convention calls for the title to be roughly in the center of the page, with your name, the professor's name, course title, and date all beneath.

mudlark: someone who scavenges in river mud for items of value

TIPS FOR DIFFERENT TYPES OF PAPERS

The diversity of your course schedule requires an equal diversity in the papers you'll write during your college career. The methods of constructing a political science paper, for example, will vary from the approaches to art history papers. All papers, however, must be well written. That is, they must have a cohesive purpose, solid, accurate evidence to support it, sound grammar, style, and clarity (basically, everything we've harped on in this book).

This chapter examines some details of writing papers for specific classes. If you've never written a paper in a particular field, be sure to ask your professor for a sample essay or some assignment guidelines. This example will indicate your professor's expectations of a well-written paper. Knowing what your professor expects will help you to approach your assignment.

In the following sections, we will discuss some specific paper types you might encounter in different subject areas. While we offer some tips and pointers on what to look for, it's obvious that all papers will not conform to these molds. As always, your professor is the one giving you a grade. Make sure you're clear about what he or she expects.

PHILOSOPHY PAPERS

Dave Barry, in his interpretation of college subjects, defines philosophy this way: "[Philosophy] involves sitting in a room and deciding there is no such thing as reality and then going to lunch. You should major in philosophy if you plan to take a lot of drugs." Since neither your professor nor you accept this position, you should lay off the drugs and learn how to write a solid philosophy paper.

Philosophy papers revolve around arguments—making them and analyzing them. When you make an argument in a philosophy paper, every premise must be explained and every step of logic must be guided. Because these new arguments require an understanding of each idea and its premise, philosophy papers *must* be clear. Your philosophy paper is not the place to show your professor that you studied for your SATs and can employ words like *gourmandize, execrate,* and *jettison.*

You will be graded on how well you scrutinize, defend, or criticize arguments, not on how mellifluous your prose is or how well you echo the professor's ideas. Writing what you think your professor wants to hear will not earn you an A. Professors would rather see that you understand the ideas well enough to make bold, well-constructed critiques of your own.

> Think of yourself as writing for a sort of "ideal reader"—someone who reads everything you write with an open mind but a very critical eye. Assume only what you think no one could deny without unreasonable prejudice and challenge anything that you think does not meet such a high standard.
>
> —Michael P. Wolf, Professor of Philosophy, Georgetown University

fud: a rabbit's or hare's tail

When writing your philosophy paper, make sure it includes the following five elements:

1. *A clear exposition and a statement of the argument in question.* You should alert the reader of your argument in your introduction, but you should mention the argument often to keep your reader engaged and to ensure that your writing is clear.

2. *A clear statement of how you will argue.* Your introduction should include not only a thesis, but a detailed description of the path your argument will take. Lay out what you plan to prove, and how you will go about proving it. Explicitly reference this map of your arguments throughout the paper. Topic sentences or statements should refer to this map.

3. *A round of defense or criticism.* When you defend or criticize, try to avoid generalizations. If you try to disprove the idea that "Tic-Tacs make your breath smell fresh," the argument that "The kid who sits behind me in calculus has bad breath after he downs 5 Tic-Tacs" is more convincing than "some people still have bad breath after they eat the mints."

4. *An opportunity for the other side of the argument to reply.* Forecast the criticism of your reader. You might think of a way of defending your Tic-Tac thesis against the reader's possible claim that evaluating freshness of breath is an arbitrary measurement.

5. *A final, deciding round of criticism or replies from your view.* Here is where you convince your reader that your rationale is superior to any criticisms. This information is generally contained in your concluding paragraph.

Criticizing an Argument

There are generally two strong ways to criticize an argument. You can show that one of the argument's premises is false, or show that the argument's logic is unsound. Using *counterexamples* can disprove certain premises or logic.

Example: Suppose a brilliant philosopher makes the claim, "All dining hall food tastes like cardboard." The T-bone steak and shrimp on Parents' Weekend is a counterexample. Even though the dining hall food is edible for only one meal each year, this counterexample proves that the original claim is faulty.

Make sure you assert *only* what you are ready to defend thoroughly. In an field where one faulty premise invalidates an entire theory, you must make sure there are no weak points that receive less attention. The length of your paper will dictate the number of claims you can defend thoroughly. Jeanine Diller from Seattle Pacific University tells her philosophy students: "If your paper is short (four to five pages), you may want to develop and use only your strongest point for your view, and reply to only the strongest objection against your view. If the paper is longer, develop more points for and against. But, overall, strive for depth over breadth."

The Use of *I*

Ask your professor about using the first person before you submit the essay. Some professors allow you to say things like "I am going to prove," but others hold to the idea that the subjective *I* should never appear in academic writing.

ENGLISH PAPERS

Dave Barry's idea of English: "[English] involves writing papers about long books you have read little snippets of just before class. Here is a tip on how to get good grades on your English papers: Never say anything about a book that anybody with any common sense would say. For example, suppose you are studying *Moby-Dick*. Anybody with any common sense would say that Moby-Dick is a big white whale, since the characters in the book refer to it as a big white whale roughly eleven thousand times. So in your paper, you say Moby-Dick is actually the Republic of Ireland. Your professor, who is sick to death of reading papers and never liked *Moby-Dick* anyway, will think you are enormously creative. If you can regularly come up with lunatic interpretations of simple stories, you should major in English."

berk or burk: a fool

Literature Essays

- Include the title and author of the book in the introductory paragraph.
- Use present tense. (Remember, unlike history narratives, these essays do not always require chronological examples.)
- The topic sentences in these papers should be placed at the beginning of each paragraph. (This rule doesn't always apply in other subjects.)

Overdoing the quotes is suspect. If half of "your" paper involves the author's quotes, the professor will suspect that a) you skimmed the book while catching the "Who Needs the Kwik-E-Mart" episode of *The Simpsons* or b) that you are too stupid to come up with your own words. Note: Neither a) nor b) are desirable suspicions for your grade-giving professor to have.

Quotes, however, *should* be used. Unless their context is obvious (most people know that "it was the best of times, it was the worst of times" is the beginning of *Tale of Two Cities*), try to inform your reader of the context. If a description of the context requires a long explanation or detracts from your argument, don't bother including it.

Replace some of your words with short quotes. Remember that the authors of the books you read are more respected than you. No matter how convinced you are that your professor loves you and the apples that you bring her everyday, she most likely appreciates the words of Dickens over yours.

Avoid all author adulation. Praise for the brilliance of James Joyce will not compensate for a weak paper; instead, it will waste your reader's time. Praising the brilliance of your professor or teaching assistant, however, is another story....

Poetry

Generally, an essay analyzing poetry will include a volley of observations that justify a thesis.

Avoid the "the poet says that" approach. Instead, consider referring to the poet as the "speaker" or the "persona." An insightful analysis will provide you with other ways of referring to the author. You could refer to the voice in one of Shakespeare's sonnets as "the lover." Don't shy away from being descriptive or creative in referencing the poet. Consider Shel Silverstein's *The Sitter*.

> Mrs. McTwitter the baby-sitter,
> I think she's a little bit crazy.
> She thinks a baby-sitter's supposed
> To sit upon the baby.

In your scholarly analysis of this poem, you could refer to the author as "the incredulous child." After completing this paper, you should consider dropping out of the University of Peachtree and transferring to a school with a slightly more challenging curriculum.

Likewise, avoid the "this poem is" approach. Instead, refer to it by its title and/or a short description. Example: "The Sitter" or "the narrative of a confused child" or "Silverstein's work" are preferred over "this poem."

Keep the quotes short. Brevity is especially key in short poems.

Questions to consider when professors give you the ever-specific "Write about your favorite poem" topic.

What audience does the voice address? The self? A particular individual? Humankind in general? An abstraction? A disobedient cocker spaniel?

defenestration: (an act of) flinging someone out a window

What tone marks the poem and how does it influence the meaning or message of the poem? Is it objective, defensive, withdrawn, or madder than your roommate after you've hit your snooze button 25 times? How does the language create tone? Is it monosyllabic or polysyllabic, descriptive or simple, sensory or nonsensory, monotone or emphatic?

Is there an identifiable structural pattern? Some poems follow a stanzas pattern; others have continuous form (blank verse, terza rima); others follow fixed form (sonnet, villanelle, rondeau).

Odds are, you'll discuss what to include in class. Your professor might elaborate about some of the above terms, or add ideas of his or her own.

WRITING ABOUT FILM

Writing your first paper in Film Studies 101 might feel weird. Unlike a history, science, or English paper, but similar to an art history paper, a paper on film requires that you comment on what you see instead of what evidence you read. Because a film's thesis is not clearly delineated, identifying themes and formulating arguments presents a challenge.

Here are some questions to consider when analyzing a film sequence:

How is **camera placement** and **movement** used in the sequence? How does the angle of camera placement (high-angle, low-angle) affect the meaning of individual shots? Does the camera remain in one position, or is it handheld, tracked, or panned?

How does **sound** affect the mood or the theme? Why is sound manipulation (echoes, for example) or music used in a particular scene?

How is **editing** used in the sequence? How does the order of unrelated shots affect the meaning or mood?

How is **acting** used in the sequence? Do certain body movements or facial expressions reveal any themes in the plot?

ART HISTORY

An art history paper differs from a history paper in that the analysis of art involves what you see. What makes writing an essay on art a challenge is the translation of the visual (the painting) into the verbal (your brilliant essay). This translation requires an understanding of the language of the discipline. Look at your assigned reading to find the art jargon that art historians employ or check out art dictionaries. Online art dictionaries also allow you to load up on vocabulary that convinces people you know what you're talking about. Even more preferable than an art dictionary is picking up on the art jargon that your professor uses in lecture. Using a term or phrase your professor has coined brings bonus points.

Offer description of the painting, but make sure the observations deliver an argument and support a thesis. Professors don't appreciate haphazard checklists of observations (he can see the painting too), even if they include cool art terminology like *chiaroscuro* and *leitmotif*. Likewise, professors do not appreciate analytical papers that fail to include specific observations. When you go to the museum to examine the artwork or when you look at a reproduction of it in a textbook, make sure you note specific examples that you can include in your paper.

Unlike history or English papers, art history papers may be structured so that the topic sentence falls at the end of the sentence. The preceding portion of the paragraph should build up an idea by giving observations about the material, color, light, style, or composition.

Avoid the subjective "I" at all costs. This advice applies to all academic writing, but looking at art often invites the student to comment, "I think that…"

zarf oer **zurf:** an ornamental holder for a hot coffee cup

Art history professors consider the following words as inappropriate to scholarly art history papers:

- *Piece*—this word tends to be overused. Professors prefer that you refer to the art according to its medium (painting, sculpture, print).
- *Palate*—don't make your teacher think you're an idiot by talking about the roof of your mouth. *Palette* is the correct spelling.

Make sure you tell the reader important dates (i.e., the date of the work's completion).

Categories of Paper Assignments

While most papers will include elements of a couple of the categories, understanding these general groupings will better understand the assignment.

Formal Analysis

This question asks for a detailed description of the formal aspects of art. Your description should include observations of design qualities like composition, color, line, texture, proportion, continuity, balance, size, and contrast. How specific your observations need to be is generally determined by the length of the assignment. Most art history papers combine some elements of formal analysis with the other categories of art history papers.

Style Analysis

This category requires observation of the art's relation to a particular stylistic category. Is the painting impressionistic, modern, early Macedonian, or Renaissance? Professors enjoy assigning essays that ask you to compare and contrast two pieces of art from the same or different styles, since this type of analysis requires you to observe the broader trends of art. Questions like "How does your five-year-old brother's finger painting differ from the finger painting that Picasso designed when he was five?" or "Compare and contrast the impressionism of Monet with that of Morisot" or "Can Caravaggio's work be classified as still life?" require a stylistic analysis.

Iconography

Literally, iconography means "image writing." This paper requires you to examine the symbolism of certain objects. Does the hammer and sickle that Mona Lisa carries reveal anything about Da Vinci's political leanings? (One should note that Mona Lisa's hammer and sickle are, technically, imaginary icons concocted by the authors of this book. Da Vinci's painting dates at 1506, more than three hundred years before communist ideas were contrived.)

Iconology

Literally, this term means "image study." When you write this type of art history paper, you will examine literary and outside texts to interpret the images in the art. This essay might require that you read the ancient Greek myths and explain how symbols in archaic Greek art allude to those myths.

Patronage Study

In this paper, the history of the actual work of art and its patron are researched. Instructors generally expect that such papers comment on political, economic, and social state during the period when the art was designed, purchased, discarded, or renewed.

HISTORY PAPERS (or Sociology or Anthropology)

The history paper differs from other academic papers because it involves 1) the transformation of facts into evidence, and 2) the transformation of evidence into an argument. The solid history paper will offer insightful interpretations of the evidence.

Generally, historical writing involves the analysis of primary or secondary sources. References to the primary sources should be considered chronologically, while references to secondary sources need not be structured in sequential order. Instead, essays on secondary sources should be ordered by ideas and logic.

> **cloop:** the sound of drawing a cork from a bottle

When gathering your historical information, consider the biases and validity of your sources. If you happened to be writing about the history of high-school truancy, you might be tempted to reference the movie *Ferris Bueller's Day Off*. But, alas, Ferris's account is biased towards the student view and fails to give the hapless principal's perspective.

When considering the viability of sources, look at the author's footnotes. Footnotes that have very few resources or resources from only one standpoint (i.e., only students' accounts) help reveal the author's bias. Another benefit of scouring the footnotes is finding information that will alert you to other good sources to consider.

Don't fall into the trap of narrating. You're not telling a story, you're explaining ideas such as "Why is this story relevant to other historical matters?" Make sure not to add superfluous facts or irrelevant data; they merely distract from the ideas you're trying to convey. While it might be interesting, the outfit that Ben Stein wore the day Ferris skipped school is not of absolute importance to the story. Interesting but irrelevant facts do not belong in your paper; tell them to your roommate.

A good history paper will examine the context of a quote or piece of evidence. Taking quotes out of context can misrepresent an author's meaning. Although fragments of sentences may be pulled from the texts you are analyzing, you must convey the entire idea and not just the select phrase. For example, let's say an author writes a sentence like, "While Shakespeare enjoyed video games like *The Legend of Zelda*, he much preferred board games like Monopoly." To write in an essay that "Shakespeare 'enjoyed video games like *Zelda* more than anything else'" misrepresents the author. Don't try to construct quotes that fit your explanation; include their entire ideas and make sure they are entirely accurate. Professors who can identify quotes that have misconstrued the source will severely penalize your paper.

When writing a history paper, avoid phrases like "since the beginning of time" or "history has shown." Such colloquial generalizations annoy professors. Be insightful and give your reader a condensed explanation of the context of the evidence.

Use the past tense. This is history, remember? Also, remember to avoid using the subjective *I*.

walty: inclined to lean or roll over

ESSAY EXAMS

Research indicates that blue books are second to the rack as forms of torture. (Most) professors, however, do not intend these essay exams to induce sweat and nervous breakdowns; instead, they use the essay exam as a learning device. Perhaps it's surprising, but teachers do not get sadistic satisfaction from your failure. In fact, your performance serves as some measure of their success in teaching the information thoroughly.

WHY DO PROFESSORS GIVE THEM?

While professors assign out-of-class papers so you can learn more about a related topic, the essay exam demonstrates that you've already learned the topics discussed in lectures. Your professor assigns essay exams to determine how well you have absorbed a body of information, how insightfully you can eliminate the less important information, and how concisely you can explain the relevance of the information. Essay exams tell the professor that:

You understand the basic concepts of the course.

- Can you compare and contrast the evidence, draw connections, identify relationships, note anomalies, and recall evidence?

You can synthesize the facts given in lecture, in readings, and in discussion sections.

- Can you organize the ideas coherently, eliminating the extraneous facts, figures, and concepts?

You can create and support an argument with the information gleaned from the course.

- Have you developed a critical and analytical approach to information?

Professor William Woodward of Seattle Pacific University gives some advice on preparing for and taking an essay exam:

> Most essays could be expanded to book length: Don't try! Most essays tempt you to plunge right in and ramble on until the time expires or you run out of ideas: Don't yield! Most essays offer an opportunity for a glittering generalization: Be specific instead! Most essays conceal several individual subpoints: Answer the whole question and nothing but the question!

Should accomplishing such a lofty task seem like an insurmountable feat, Professor Woodward recommends five steps to writing an excellent essay exam:

1. Prepare: *Study* with the essay requirement in mind.

2. Peruse: *Read* the question, making sure to look at the time allotted and the information requested.

3. Ponder: *Analyze* the content of the question.

4. Plan: *Organize* your response.

5. Proceed: *Write!*

lethologica: a mental block for certain words

HOW CAN YOU BE A PREPARED EXAM TAKER?

The most crucial time of preparation is during the semester. Go to lectures (leaving your calculator games at home). Do at least *some* of the reading. The more you read, the more you'll understand, and the more you'll recall when blue-book mania comes around. Participate in your discussion sections; it forces you to consider the material ahead of time. (For another thing, section performance also serves as an indication to the professor of how well you understand. The impact you make during discussion sections, therefore, can affect his idea of your essay performance). Take good notes.

As the dreaded exam date nears, avoid haphazard memorization. If the professor has given you the essay questions beforehand, rejoice, do an Irish jig, and begin outlining information. Know, however, that professors who assign the questions ahead of time expect essays that are more organized with more information than those essays composed without previous preparation.

Try to organize the information by theme. Capture each theme by writing it out in one sentence. Next to that sentence, list a couple examples or facts that support the claim you're making. Even if the essays are not supplied in advance, this preparation tool helps you recall broad categories. When you see the question that might involve one of the broad categories you've prepared, you will be ready to list the relevant evidence and information.

Anticipate potential questions and prepare accordingly. If your professor has dedicated three lectures to the role of parakeets in the Persian Gulf War, expect that there will be a question that asks you something like "explain the relevance of parakeets in that quick American victory."

Working in study groups allows you to collectively brainstorm potential questions and cement ideas. Practice communicating your ideas to classmates, and you will be better prepared to communicate your ideas to your grader.

HOW SHOULD YOU GO ABOUT TAKING THE TEST?

I initially write an outline consisting of a thesis sentence, supporting topic sentences, and short notes following each topic sentence. I find that this method is particularly effective for essays that are based on substance and not style. A structured, straightforward response to the question regardless of style or technique will usually generate a better grade than a free-style response. Graders generally look for specific points and grade higher on essays that are clear and concise. I divide the time up by the number of questions and the relative level of difficulty of each question. More time should be allotted for the more difficult questions, and less time should be allotted for the easier questions. I write the topic sentences for paragraphs and, depending on the time remaining, list the key points under each paragraph.

—Helen Jen, Cornell University, computer science major

Before you get the test, consider how much time you have. If you know there will be twenty essays that you have to write in ten hours, you will know to limit each essay to half an hour. Write the time you should be finished with each section so that you can quickly compare your progress with the clock. Nothing's worse than leaving out an entire section because you've spent too long elaborating on the camouflaged feathers of parakeets in the Persian Gulf War.

Once you get the exam, read it carefully. Do not neglect reading the instructions! If you have a choice in questions, consider which question you are best prepared to answer. If you're not prepared to answer any of the questions because hysteria has hit and your mind has gone blank, calm down. Read the questions again. Consider one question at a time. Breathe.

> **kang:** a Chinese sleeping platform that can be warmed by a fire underneath

The first thing I do when I get an in-class essay question in front of me is take a deep breath. There is nothing more important than being relaxed and collected when time is ticking and pressure is rising. Next, I use a scrap piece of paper (or the assignment/exam itself) and make an outline. Jumping in before my thoughts and information are organized is a big waste of time. The introduction and conclusion are pretty straight forward once I decide what my argument or hypothesis will be. The paragraphs in between must each contain valuable support and examples. Their order must be logical and easy to follow. Once I have this framework, writing is easy—I just bang out one paragraph at a time. If I start running out of time, I stick to the bare essentials and throw on a conclusion that consists of a paraphrase of my introduction. Then I turn it in and take another deep breath.

—Samantha Coren Spitzer, Brown
University, sociology major

When you look at each question, consider each element of the question. Numbering each element helps too. Underline key words.

In your nervousness and time-rushed state, do not neglect making an outline. Not only will this preparation provide an organized response, but when random ideas come into your mind, you can jot them down in your outline and remember to include them later. Your outline need not be perfectly structured or impeccably detailed. All that is important is that your outline affords you a workable strategy and helps you remember key ideas. Professor Ward of the University of Southern California explains the importance of outlining before writing:

Coherence and flow (transitions) are important for in-class essays. Students should take a few minutes to make a brief outline for each essay of the major points and supporting evidence. This outline can be left in the margin of the first page of the essay so that the teacher can see that the student is well organized.

—Thomas W. Ward, Anthropology Lecturer,
University of Southern California

Tips on Beating the Clock

If you run out of time on an in-class essay, you can conclude by quickly outlining the rest of what you wanted to say. This way, you can fit two or three paragraphs into a few sentences. Depending on the professor, you might get more credit than if you had just ended midthought, with an incomplete essay. It shows you at least had a few more things to discuss, and that you were not just sitting there daydreaming or wracking your brain for a way to end.

—Anne Rittman, Georgetown University,
English/history major

I always outline in order to organize my thoughts first. I constantly watch the clock in order to keep track of time. If I only have two minutes and two paragraphs left, I just write like a maniac and try to finish as much as possible.

—Stephanie Howard, Colorado University,
psychology major

On a timed essay or exam, the temptation is great to avoid an outline because it is seen as taking away moments from the actual drafting of one's response. In reality, an outline is an anchor, even a security blanket, that frames our writing with unity and succinctness. The five minutes or so required for its creation repays the writer in cogency many times over.

—Stephen M. Byars, associate director of
the writing program, University of Southern
California

Remind yourself of your common mistakes before you begin writing. For example, if you always forget to paragraph, then write ****PARA-GRAPH**** on the top of the page. (But make sure you erase it before you hand it in. :)).

—Marianne Yip, Princeton University

book scorpion: a scorpionlike arachnid found in libraries, probably feeding on booklice

I find it helpful to jot down everything that comes to mind on scrap paper, then look at what I have and decide how to either organize it or fit it into a coherent essay. I see if my list can be subdivided, and then I put numbers next to the items to mark some kind of order. Finally, I write the essay. This is almost the same as making the outline, but sometimes I get stuck trying to start from the beginning of an outline without thinking of the ideas that will be included.

I usually write as fast as I can, and then spend the rest of the time proofreading. I might even rewrite the essay. I think that once they've started writing, most people come up with information fast enough to write it all down quickly, and if this is not done sometimes ideas are lost or the writer gets caught in a blank space.

I write some sort of topic sentence for the first paragraph, skip a few lines, and then do the same for the second. Chances are, if you've got two paragraphs left, the last one will be a "conclusion" paragraph that ties together the ideas in your essay. It's very important to include this paragraph, so I find that this method is the best.

—Stephanie Obodda, Princeton University

I initially write an outline consisting of a thesis sentence, supporting topic sentences, and short notes following each topic sentence. I find that his method is particularly effective for essays that are based on substance and not style. A structured, straightforward response to the question regardless of style or technique will usually generate a better grade than a freestyle response. Graders generally look for specific points and grade higher on essays that are clear and concise. I divide the time up by the number of questions and the relative level of difficulty of each question. More time should be allotted for the more difficult questions, and less time should be allotted for the easier questions. I write the topic sentence for both paragraphs and, depending on the time remaining, list the key points under each paragraph.

—Helen Jen, Cornell Senior, computer science major

I see exactly what the question is asking, then I think for a minute or two about the question and how I am going to answer it. Then write. I usually restate the question in an answer form in my first sentence. Essay questions generally cover larger topics or major themes studied in a course, and by taking good notes during class sessions, doing the assigned reading, and putting in the hours before the test studying, I try not be caught off guard by any essay question. It always helps to be familiar with the material so you do not waste time trying to recall something. Instead you have the ability to write it down, and keep moving.

Wear a watch! NO alarm: You don't want to piss off a neighbor. Teachers usually will announce when there is something like 10 minutes or five minutes left. If this really helps you, ask the teacher beforehand if they can make such an announcement.

I write slowly; it has been an Achilles heel throughout college . . . Try not to panic. Write down notes, key words, themes, that you would have written down if you had more time. Write "time" on the test so the prof knows that you ran out. My experience is that if you have done good work up until the point when the tests are collected, demonstrating that you know, understand, and can critically and intelligently discuss the material, then most profs are sympathetic at grading the part of the test that you didn't complete. Writing fast and not wasting time always helps on tests, but some of us are slow with our pens. You need to ask yourself if the test was really too long?—were there other kids writing frantically at the end of the test period too? or were you there because you weren't well prepared so that you could answer the questions accurately and with speed. Ask the prof In advance if the class can begin five minutes early if he or she feels like the test might be long.

—Ian R. Broennle, Davidson College,
German major

jubate: very hairy

When you crack open the blue book, make sure to put the number of your essay on the top of the page. It saves the professor time and energy, and you want a happy grader.

Write your thesis first. Depending on the expected length of the essay, you may not need a long introduction. If you've outlined your answer and summarized that outline in your introduction, however, the teacher will be more cognizant of the organization and he might even give you partial credit for those points you did not have time to cover.

A final small but important detail: Consider writing double-spaced. If your paper is double-spaced, and you realize that you've forgotten to mention some fact after you've completed a paragraph, it's easier to go back and put it back in. Professors appreciate neat exams.

CONCLUSION

We hope this book has provided you with at least a couple of hints that will help improve that History 220 paper, and maybe it's even given you a greater appreciation for the struggles of the common wombat. Equipped with the greatest techniques for researching, outlining, drafting, and editing that American academia can offer, you are now prepared to join the ranks of William Shakespeare, Charles Dickens, F. Scott Fitzgerald, and Herman Melville, all of whom also read our book and found it extraordinarily helpful.

But let's be honest: We know that implementing these techniques is easier said than done, especially when you've got *The Simpsons* to watch, a ton assigned by Professor Good-Thing-You-Don't-Have-Any-Other-Classes (not his real name) to read, and the *Who Wants to Be a Millionaire* hotline to call. But we also know that writing a good paper is not an insurmountable feat, even for the busiest of students. Take Justin for example. He's training nonstop for the World's Strongest Man competition, but you don't hear him complaining about the thirteen classes he took this semester (Editor's note: He's lying. Ignore him). Remember, no formula can guarantee improvement, but every literate student is capable of it.

Now you've perused the pages of this book, and you've been able to see what tactics have worked for other students. Using their experience as a starting point, go find your own technique for success. Thank you and goodnight.